Volume 31

A HISTORY OF
PERSONNEL ADMINISTRATION
1890 TO 1910

A HISTORY OF PERSONNEL ADMINISTRATION 1890 TO 1910

OSCAR W. NESTOR

Routledge
Taylor & Francis Group

LONDON AND NEW YORK

First published in 1986 by Garland Publishing, Inc.

This edition first published in 2017
by Routledge
2 Park Square, Milton Park, Abingdon, Oxon OX14 4RN

and by Routledge
711 Third Avenue, New York, NY 10017

Routledge is an imprint of the Taylor & Francis Group, an informa business

British Library Cataloguing in Publication Data
A catalogue record for this book is available from the British Library

ISBN: 978-1-138-80870-6 (Set)
ISBN: 978-1-315-18006-9 (Set) (ebk)
ISBN: 978-0-415-78675-1 (Volume 31) (hbk)
ISBN: 978-0-415-78679-9 (Volume 31) (pbk)
ISBN: 978-1-315-22670-5 (Volume 31) (ebk)

Publisher's Note
The publisher has gone to great lengths to ensure the quality of this reprint but
points out that some imperfections in the original copies may be apparent.

Disclaimer
The publisher has made every effort to trace copyright holders and would welcome
correspondence from those they have been unable to trace.

A HISTORY OF PERSONNEL ADMINISTRATION
1890 TO 1910

Oscar W. Nestor

Garland Publishing, Inc.
New York & London ★ 1986

Library of Congress Cataloging-in-Publication Data

Nestor, Oscar W.
  A history of personnel administration, 1890 to 1910.

  (American business history)
  Thesis (doctoral)—University of Pennsylvania.
  1. Personnel management—United States—History.
I. Title. II. Series.
HF5549.2.U5N5 1986   658.3'00973   86-9944
ISBN 0-8240-8365-2

INTRODUCTION

This study is an attempt to examine and evaluate the personnel techniques and activities that were characteristic of one
period in American industrial life. In later years these techniques
and activities came to be known as personnel management or personnel administration. By these terms is meant the policies, procedures, and programs that were introduced by companies for the
purpose of bringing about constructive and harmonious relationships
between management and its own employees. The great majority of
companies which introduced these programs did not deal with outside
labor organizations. As a result, this movement, except in isolated
cases, did not deal with the problems that arise under union management relations.

The period selected comprises the two decades beginning in
1890. It is felt that an historical study of personnel programs
and policies has distinct merit since an understanding of the
history of a movement is required in order to comprehend and to
appraise intelligently its present day functions and probable
development. A knowledge of what employers actually did to improve conditions of industrial relations and the successes and
failures of earlier years provide an invaluable handbook of
experience for the understanding and solution of modern problems.

The period 1890 to 1910 has been singled out for special
study because many of the present day personnel functions were
initiated or subjected to experimentation during these years.

Although this period was relatively devoid of the drastic innovations of the nineteen thirties, new ideas did emerge and existing
programs were refined. This study will isolate and study these
programs. In those cases where specific motives for employers'
actions can be determined, these motives will be set forth. In
ascertaining the new techniques and programs that were introduced
and the extent to which existing ones were accelerated and modified, consideration will be given to (1) the quantitative increase or decrease of such activities, (2) the factors that led
to their introduction, (3) the degree to which employees participated in decisions related to the initiation and administration of
personnel activities, (through unions, employee representation
plans, or suggestion systems), and (4) the impact of federal and
state legislation on these programs. This study is concerned
with the development of personnel administration, that is to say,
with policies and programs initiated and administered by employers.
For that reason, this thesis will not deal with the labor movement except when that movement had a direct impact on the rise
and development of personnel functions and activities. It should
be noted, as pointed out later, that fewer than one out of every
ten employees were members of labor organizations as late as
1910.

Since no analysis of the changes in personnel activity
would be possible unless practices prior to 1890 were known,
some research has also been conducted in this area. Despite the
paucity of concrete, quantitative information regarding personnel

activity, both prior to and during this period, an effort has been made to summarize and classify the information by specific activity.

The information embodied in this study was obtained from governmental publications, particularly of the Department of Commerce and the Department of Labor; the writings of private individuals in the contemporary literature of the period, and private, unpublished material which was made available to the writer.

The writer is deeply grateful to various members of the faculty of the Wharton School of Finance and Commerce for their help and suggestions. Special gratitude is due Dr. Anne Bezanson for her contributions to the initial planning and organization of this study. Dr. Waldo E. Fischer furnished invaluable advice and counsel in all problems associated with the study. His guidance at crucial moments will always be remembered. Dr. Rexford B. Hersey also reviewed the completed manuscript.

Grateful acknowledgment is also extended to Mrs. Jane D. Clark who was untiring in her efforts in the preparation of the manuscript.

To my wife, for her constant patience and words of encouragement, this study is humbly dedicated.

Corning, New York   Oscar W. Nestor
April 11, 1954.

CONTENTS

CHAPTER I

ECONOMIC SETTING

To understand a movement, it is necessary to study it within the context of the forces and conditions which prevailed at the time and greatly influenced its development. This chapter, therefore, will attempt to highlight the important economic developments which influenced the rise of personnel administration. The period under study was an era of marked industrial development, heavy immigration, a shifting population and, after 1898, a slow, upward movement of wages and prices. Organized labor had withstood the great depression of the nineties without a decline in its total membership and was actively engaged in expanding its membership and in obtaining wider recognition. Personnel efforts naturally reflected these changes and conditions. A more careful examination of the prevailing economic climate, therefore, is a part of the task which has been undertaken.

General Economic Conditions

Because over-all economic conditions greatly influence the actions of employers, this presentation begins with an analysis of business activity in this period. The level of business activity by individual years, as determined by Willard L. Thorp, is shown in Table I.[1]

---

1 Mr. Thorp bases his determination on a careful analysis of production, price movements, interest rates, and other economic indicators.

Table I

Economic Conditions in the United States, 1890-1909, inclusive[1]

Year	Nature of Economic Activity	Year	Nature of Economic Activity
1890	Prosperity and recession	1900	Prosperity; brief recession
1891	Prosperity and recession	1901	Prosperity
1892	Prosperity	1902	Prosperity
1893	Panic; depression	1903	Prosperity; recession
1894	Deep depression	1904	Mild depression; revival
1895	Depression; revival	1905	Prosperity
1896	Recession; depression	1906	Prosperity
1897	Depression; revival	1907	Prosperity; panic; depression
1898	Revival; prosperity	1908	Depression
1899	Prosperity	1909	Revival; mild prosperity

[1] Taken from Thorp, Willard L., Business Annals (New York: National Bureau of Economic Research, Inc., 1926), pp. 136-41.

In general, the first three years in the nineties were mildly prosperous. The succeeding five years may be characterized as a period of severe depression, broken only by a brief revival in the latter half of 1895. The country then experienced over-all prosperity through 1909, with only brief exceptions in 1903-04 and again in 1907-08. Industrial production was at least equal to or above the trend line in eleven of the twenty years under examination.[2]

During these years, the cost of living was subject to drastic fluctuations. Table II discloses a decline in living costs during the first half of the nineties. Thereafter, except for a slight

[2] Using only industrial production as a barometer, production was above or equal to the normal trend line in eleven of the 20 years. Those years were 1890, 1892, 1898-1902, inclusive, 1905-1907, inclusive, and 1909. Bowman, Mary Jean and Bach, George L., Economic Analysis and Public Policy (New York: Prentice-Hall, Inc., 1949), p. 215.

drop in 1903-1904, and a more substantial one in 1908-1909, these prices tended toward higher levels. In 1909, the index of cost of living stood at 121 as compared with 104 in 1890 and 97 in 1894-1895. The high point of the period occurred in 1907 when the index reached 126.

Table II

Index of Living Costs in Non-agricultural Areas, 1890-1909, inclusive[1]

Year	Index of Living Costs	Year	Index of Living Costs
1890	104	1900	106
1891	101	1901	108
1892	102	1902	111
1893	100	1903	116
1894	97	1904	115
1895	97	1905	115
1896	99	1906	119
1897	100	1907	126
1898	100	1908	121
1899	102	1909	121

[1] 1890 - 99 = 100. Taken from Douglas, Paul H., Real Wages in the United States, 1890-1926 (Boston: Houghton, Mifflin Company, 1930), p. 60.

Table III shows the average annual earnings and the trend of money and real earnings for this twenty-year period. By 1909, average annual earnings had increased to $594 as compared to $486 in 1890. Most of this increase came in the first decade of the twentieth century; the previous ten years having been character- ized by an uneven decline in earnings. The rise which started in 1898 pushed annual money earnings to a level that was 25 per cent

above the ten-year base. Annual real wages, on the other hand,
moved within a very restricted range. By 1909, they had moved to
only about three per cent above the ten year base. A comparison
of annual real wage and cost-of-living data shows that real wage

Table III

Average Annual Earnings, Relative Money Earnings,
and Relative Real Earnings in All Industries, 1890-
1909, inclusive[1]

Year	Average Annual Earnings (Dollars)	Relative Annual Earnings	Relative Real Earnings
1890	$ 486	103	99
1891	487	103	102
1892	495	104	103
1893	480	101	101
1894	448	95	98
1895	468	99	102
1896	462	97	98
1897	462	97	98
1898	468	99	98
1899	480	101	99
1900	490	103	98
1901	508	107	100
1902	519	109	99
1903	543	115	99
1904	540	114	99
1905	554	117	102
1906	569	120	101
1907	595	126	100
1908	563	119	98
1909	594	125	103

[1] Taken from Douglas, Paul H., op.cit., p. 392. 1890-99=100.
Wages of farm labor are excluded.

improvement sometimes occurred when living costs fell, and, at
other times, when they rose.

Unemployment

Another factor affecting the economic status of workers was
the extent of unemployment in this period. It is quite evident
from Table IV that unemployment represented a very real problem.
Figures are not available before 1897, but in that year, more than
1.2 million people, or about 18 per cent of the working force in
manufacturing, transportation, building trades, and mining were
unemployed. In 1898, unemployment was also high. Thereafter, an

Table IV

Unemployment in Manufacturing, Transportation,
Building Trades, and Mining, 1897 to 1909, inclusive[1]

Year	Total Labor Supply (ooo omitted)	Total Unemployed (ooo omitted)	Percentage Unemployed
1897	7,015	1,266	18.0
1898	7,164	1,214	16.9
1899	7,327	766	10.5
1900	7,527	755	10.0
1901	7,805	584	7.5
1902	8,347	569	6.8
1903	8,702	609	7.0
1904	8,748	883	10.1
1905	9,349	622	6.7
1906	9,817	577	5.9
1907	10,129	695	6.9
1908	10,103	1,654	16.4
1909	10,394	925	8.9

1 Douglas, Paul H., op.cit., p. 460. It should be remembered that these
figures relate to certain industries only. It should be noted
also that they include those disabled by sickness or accident. It
is estimated that this latter group would approximate from 2 to 3
per cent of the labor supply at any given time.

uneven decline took place until 1904 when it again increased to

over 800,000 workers. Employment in these industries remained

fairly constant during the next three years. In 1908, more than
1.6 million workers, or 16 per cent of the working force, were
unemployed. The following year the unemployed numbered 925,000
and the percentage figure fell to 8.9.

Population and Immigration

Growth of Population

One of the significant characteristics of this period, which
brought both benefits and problems, was a continuation of the remarkable growth in population. An increasing population provided not
only a market for a growing production of goods and services, but
also swelled the supply of labor which had been inadequate throughout much of our country's early development. While the growth was
marked, it was at a slower rate in this twenty-year period than in
the decades immediately preceeding.[3] Table V presents population
figures for the census years of 1890, 1900, and 1910 and shows the
distribution of the population in rural and urban areas. In the
period 1890 to 1910, there was an increase of almost 30 million
people, or an average of about one and one-half million per year.
This growth in population was accompanied by an interesting shift
in its distribution. The trend toward urbanization is readily
apparent. In 1890, only about 23 million, or 36 per cent of the

---

3 Previous to 1869, the rate of increase had been more than a third
every decade; in the three decades ending in 1890, it averaged
little more than a quarter for each decade, and in the two succeeding decades, it fell to about one-fifth.

Table V

Population and its Distribution in Urban and Rural
Areas in the United States, 1890 - 1910[1]

Date	Total Population	Percent	Rural Population	Percent	Urban Population	Percent
1890	62,947,714	100.0	40,227,491	63.9	22,720,223	36.1
1900	75,994,775	100.0	45,197,390	59.5	30,797,185	40.5
1910	91,972,266	100.0	49,348,883	53.7	42,623,383	46.3

1 Lippincott, Isaac, Economic Development of the United States (New York: D. Appleton and Company, 1921), p. 313.

population, lived in urban areas as compared to 42.6 million, about 46 per cent, in 1910.

The reasons for this rather significant urbanization seem equally clear. In the first place, there was a rising demand for wage earners in manufacturing and distributive industries because of the increased demand for goods and services of a growing population. As a result, persons who wanted such work and their families were drawn to the manufacturing and commercial centers. The greater opportunities for advancement and social advantages, such as better educational facilities and more diversions, were also factors at work. In addition, newly arrived immigrants tended to settle in cities because the opportunities for ready employment were often greater there and because they could settle among friends. "Indirectly, all the forces which have promoted the growth of commerce and manufacturing are responsible for urban concentration."[4]

4 Lippincott, Isaac, op. cit., p. 312.

Immigration

One of the important factors responsible for the remarkable
increase in population during this period was the vast number of
people who migrated to the United States. Higher wages than could
be obtained abroad, a chance to get ahead, relative freedom from
class distinctions, and the opportunity to acquire land apparently
stimulated people to flock to America.

Table VI shows the volume of immigration by ten-year periods
from 1870 to 1910.

Table VI

Immigration to the United States[1]

Years	Total Immigration
1871 - 1880	2,812,191
1881 - 1890	5,246,613
1891 - 1900	3,844,420
1901 - 1910	8,795,386

1 Lippincott, Isaac, op. cit., p. 315.

In no decade prior to 1880 did the number of immigrants exceed 3
million people, but in the ten-year period ended in 1890, entries
almost doubled. After a drop in the nineties, immigration established a new record in the first decade of the nineteenth century.
The number of immigrants averaged almost 1 million people per year
in that decade. From 1891 to 1910, nearly thirteen million people
entered the United States.

An extremely important feature of immigration in this period was the change which took place in the national origin of immigrants. Previous to 1865, practically all the immigrants had come from north-western Europe, chiefly from the United Kingdom and Germany; after that date, however, there was a steadily increasing proportion of immigrants from the countries of southern and eastern Europe. This "new immigration", as it was sometimes called, included people mainly from Italy, Austria-Hungary, and Russia. "The proportion of all immigrants coming from southern and eastern Europe, never as high as three per cent until after 1870, was regularly between two-thirds and three-quarters of the total from 1898 until the war."[5] Along with the increased immigration from China and Japan, these Europeans with different institutions and backgrounds created social and economic problems and gave some cause for alarm to various groups. American labor became disturbed at the low-priced competition offered by aliens and it was during this period that exclusion legislation first appeared.

Industrial Development

The twenty-year period under consideration was one of growth in industrial activity. By 1909, agriculture was no longer our chief source of income and, internationally, we had moved rapidly toward a favorable balance of trade. There were many reasons for the far-reaching changes and developments of the period. No

---

5 Wright, Chester W., Economic History of the United States (New York: McGraw-Hill Book Company, 1941), p. 554.

longer was transportation a major obstacle to progress since, by
1890, the main outlines of the country's railroad system had been
completed. Easy access to the western half of the country, made
possible by this cheaper transportation, permitted the development
of new markets. Meanwhile, companies grew larger and more capital
was concentrated in single production units to secure the full
advantages of large output and low-unit costs. Expanding domestic
markets, concomitant improvements in processes, and the introduction
of new and better machines made such large scale production feasible.
The broad industrial changes of this period have been ably summarized by Chester W. Wright:[6]

> Favored by the continued development of the country's rich
> and varied natural resources and stimulated by the introduction
> of new machinery and the rapidly expanding domestic market,
> manufacturing grew by leaps and bounds. Before the end of the
> century manufacturing industries were making a larger net
> contribution to the national income than agriculture. Imports
> of manufactured products dwindled to only a small percentage
> of the domestic output and exports were entering the world
> markets so that in this field the country could be considered
> almost self-sufficing....By (1900) the development of the
> West had ceased to be the most important factor in shaping
> the course of events in the economic life of the nation. A
> new epoch had begun.

Table VII shows the changes which occurred in manufacturing during
this period as reported by the Bureau of the Census of the federal
government.

---

6 ibid., p. 524.

Table VII

The Growth of Manufacturing, 1890-1910[1]

Year	Number of Establish- ments	Wage Earners	Capital	Value of Products
1890	355,405	4,251,535	$ 6,525,050,759	$ 9,372,378,843
1900	207,514	4,712,763	8,975,256,496	11,406,926,701
1910	268,491	6,615,046	18,428,269,706	20,672,051,870

[1] Department of Commerce, Bureau of the Census, Biennial Census of Manufactures (Washington: Government Printing Office, 1924), p. 13. As to the comparison of the returns for the different years, the census reports make the following comment: "The statistics of manufactures secured at the decennial censuses from 1850 to 1900, inclusive, covered the neighborhood, hand, and building industries, as well as the factory industries while the reports of 1904 and 1909 were confined to factory industries."

The changes that occurred in manufacturing during these years were substantial. Despite the fact that the 1890 coverage included not only factories but neighborhood, hand, and building industries, the number of wage earners increased from almost 4.3 million to more than 6.6 million. At the same time, the amount of capital employed in manufacturing jumped from about 6.5 billion dollars to over 18.4 billion dollars. Meanwhile, the dollar value of all manu- factured products had more than doubled. The trend in the number of establishments for the period as a whole has little significance since the year 1890 included establishments other than factories. It will be noted that the number of establishments increased about 30 per cent between 1900 and 1910. Table VIII is presented to show the changes in average product, capital employed, and number of wage earners per establishment. The reader is cautioned that the data for 1890 are not strictly comparable with those for later years.

Table VIII

Average Product, Capital and Wage Earners
Per Establishment, 1890 - 1910[1]

Year	Product (ooo omitted)	Capital (ooo omitted)	Wage Earners
1890	$ 28,070	$ 19,020	13.8
1900	25,418	19,269	10.4
1910	76,993	68,638	24.6

1 Lippincott, Isaac, op. cit., p. 476.

These figures, despite their limitations, do convey some idea of the changes which took place in manufactuirng during these decades. It is apparent that the establishments were growing in size as measured by average number of workers employed, capital used, and, since cost of living only increased by 28 per cent in this period, by volume and/or quality of goods produced. These developments undoubtedly had an important impact on the industrial relations of the period, particularly since these years witnessed the growth of corporations operated by hired management. "Absentee ownership" also increased during these years.

The forces and conditions which brought about these changes were varied. They included, as pointed out earlier, the widening of markets through improved transportation and communication systems, the growth in population which created both markets and a labor force, technological changes, and the exploitation of rich natural resources. Another contributing factor was the growing use of the corporate form of business enterprise which made it possible to assemble large amounts of capital under the direction of a single company. This form of business organization was encouraged by the passage of general incorporation laws. Although incorporation laws had been passed in most states by 1860, a special charter had to be secured from the legislature before the business could be organized. In 1888, however, the State of New Jersey enacted a general incorporation law which eliminated the need for a special charter. This type of legislation, which quickly spread to other states, was a vital stimulus to the use of this legal device after 1890. The adoption of additional financial techniques, such as the holding company and the trust, also facilitated the formation of giant industrial combinations.

The industrial development of this period was responsible for numerous benefits including many new and better products, more employment and surprising stability in real wages despite some year-to-year fluctuations. But the results of these industrial changes were not altogether beneficial. On this point, Chester W. Wright wrote:[7]

> But the spread of modern capitalistic industry
> created new problems that assumed a steadily
> increasing prominence in the economic and political

---

7 Wright, Chester W., op. cit., p. 524.

life of the nation. These involved the relation
between labor and capital, the regulation of
railroads and public utilities, the control of
combinations and trusts, and the business cycle.
These problems loomed larger and more formidable
with every passing decade till, with the advent
of the 20th century, they may be said to have
become dominant issues.

Development of Unionism

Despite the panic and major depression during the years
1893 to 1898, and the opposition of powerful corporations, such
as the Carnegie Steel Company and the Pullman Company, which won
important strikes in 1892 and 1894, total union membership did
not decline. During these years "they retained close to 440,000
members." Table IX shows that after 1897 membership began to
rise with increasing momentum. In seven years, membership increased from about 440,000 to over 2 million members and the number of affiliated national unions from 58 to 220.[8] From 1904
to 1910, membership fluctuated about the two million level.

The Knights of Labor which had been a powerful labor organization in the post Civil War period and had attained a membership
of about 700,000 members in 1886, disintegrated rapidly. By 1890,
its membership had dwindled to less than 100,000 and by 1900, it
had little influence in the labor movement. The Knights were

8 Woytinsky, W.S. and Associates, Employment and Wages in the
  United States, The Twentieth Century Fund (Baltimore: The
  Lord Baltimore Press, 1953), p. 234.

Table IX

Total Membership of American Trade Unions
1897 - 1909, inclusive[1]

Year	Membership	Year	Membership
1897	447,000	1904	2,072,700
1898	500,700	1905	2,022,300
1899	611,000	1906	1,958,700
1900	868,500	1907	2,122,800
1901	1,124,700	1908	2,130,600
1902	1,375,900	1909	2,047,400
1903	1,913,900		

1 Wolman, Leo, The Growth of American Trade Unions, 1880-1923
(New York: National Bureau of Economic Research, 1924), p. 33.
Exact figures before 1897 are not available, but are believed to
have been fairly constant at about 440,000 members.

supplanted by the American Federation of Labor which was organized

along craft lines. Less idealistic than the older organization,

it placed greater emphasis upon concrete improvements for its mem-

bers. In 1893, it reported a membership of 260,000. During the

prosperity of the late nineties, it achieved considerable success

despite community opposition and the open shop drives of employers'

organizations such as the National Association of Manufacturers

and the National Metal Trades Association. In 1901, membership

had increased to over 700,000 and at the close of the period to

1,580,000.[9]

9 Morison, Samuel E., and Commager, Henry S., The Growth of the
American Republic (New York: Oxford University Press, 1942),
p. 752. Wolman estimates that in 1910, about 8.6 per cent of
the employee class belonged to a union.

Factors Influencing the Growth of the American Labor Movement

Beginning with the great anthracite coal strike in 1902, a change became evident in the attitude of many employers.[10] "Most of the powerful ones, believing that unionism was growing too strong and fearing further encroachments on their control of industry, decided to break off relations and the years from 1902 to the War were characterized by a definitely increasing anti-unionism."[11] The climate of rugged individualism and laissez-faire, which fostered the idea that a laboring man could rise by his own efforts, was not conducive to unionization nor the use of their chief weapon, the strike. After 1904 until the close of the period, total union membership showed little increase.

Despite employer opposition, powerful forces were also present to encourage the growth of the labor movement. "Among these influences, the most important were the increased mechanization of industry, the evolution of the giant corporation as an employer, the nationalization of industry and the transportation system, the decline of agriculture as a potential safety valve and the change in the character of immigration."[12] When the large corporations emerged, the bargaining power of the individual worker was correspondingly minimized and the old personal relationship between employer and employee tended to disappear. As

10 Daugherty, Carroll R., Labor Problems in American Industry (Boston: Houghton, Mifflin Company, 1948), p. 332. The first real and complete trade agreement was signed in 1891 between employers and the union in the iron-molding industry.
11 ibid., p. 333.
12 Morison, Samuel E., and Commager, Henry S., op. cit., p. 146.

the markets of these large firms expanded, the determination of
wages and other conditions of work could no longer be negotiated
on a local basis. Confronted with regional and national competition,
union organizations followed the market in which their goods and
services were sold in order to maintain labor standards. With
labor standards threatened by large numbers of immigrants, the skill
of certain crafts supplanted by machines, and the western frontier
virtually closed as an alternative for ambitious employees, the
incentive for labor organizations became more pronounced.

Labor Disputes

Several important strikes marked by violence and bloodshed
had an important effect on public opinion and created considerable
anti-labor feeling. Perhaps the most famous of these strikes were
the Haymarket Riot of 1886 in Chicago; the Homestead Strike of
1892; the Pullman Strike of 1892, and the Anthracite Strike of
1902.

Table X presents the number of work stoppages in the twenty-
year period and the number of workers involved. In 1890, the
number of work stoppages, which had risen sharply in the mid-
eighties, reached a high point. In that year, there were 1,897
strikes involving 373,000 workers. During the depression of the
nineties, the number of stoppages declined but the number of workers
involved fluctuated widely. At the turn of the century, the A.F.
of L. launched a wide-scale organizational drive which, together
with the sharp upswing of business, brought work stoppages to a new

high of over 3,600 and the number of workers involved to about 800,000. Data are not available for subsequent years in this period.

Table X

Work Stoppages in the United States, 1890 - 1905[1]

Year	Number Of Work Stoppages	Number of Workers Involved[a]	Year	Number of Work Stoppages	Number of Workers Involved[a]
1890	1,897	373	1898	1,098	263
1891	1,786	330	1899	1,838	432
1892	1,359	239	1900	1,839	568
1893	1,375	288	1901	3,012	564
1894	1,404	690	1902	3,240	692
1895	1,255	407	1903	3,648	788
1896	1,066	249	1904	2,419	574
1897	1,110	416	1905	2,186	302

a In thousands
1 Woytinsky, W.S., op. cit., p. 655.

Development of Personnel Activities

While wage earners were seeking to improve their economic status and the conditions under which they made their living through the formation of unions, some employers also sought solutions to their labor problems.

Personnel activities had not been unknown in earlier periods, but after 1890 they began to take on new meaning and were given greater emphasis. Employers here and there tried to offset the limitations of the factory system by the adoption of measures which would (1) provide greater physical comfort to their employees, and (2) ensure more harmonious employee-management relations. This movement arose partly in response to the demands of laborers for improved working conditions and for a voice in decisions about matters that affected their terms and conditions of employment. Some employers felt that such measures would promote employee loyalty, make unions less attractive, and forestall legislation on working conditions. In some instances, it was a simple expression of employer philanthropy. In part, employers were also groping for a method of promoting greater employee interest in their work, greater employee efficiency, better products at lower costs, and for a means of re-establishing the personal relationship between employer and employee that had been lost as the size of companies and establishments increased. This era of welfare work, as it has sometimes been called, included plans for the improvement of the physical conditions within an establishment, beautifying factory surroundings, provisions for housing, medical care, the organization of social clubs, training and education, incentive wage schemes, profit sharing plans, and many other activities. Many of these programs were first introduced in the period from 1890 to 1909 or achieved their first real prominence in the period under study. These personnel functions and activities will be examined in the subsequent chapters.

Summary

The twenty-year period under study was characterized by extremes in economic conditions. In the earlier years, a severe

depression greatly curtailed production, gave rise to much unemployment, and despite a decrease in the cost of living, occasioned
some decline in the real annual earnings of workers who were fortunate enough to have jobs. After 1898, business conditions,
except for two brief interruptions, improved greatly. The cost
of living rose sharply, money wages moved to higher levels, but
lagged behind the upward movement of prices throughout much of
this period. The wage increases were not substantial enough to
show material increases in real annual earnings.

Population rose at the rate of about one and one-half-million
people per year and the American people showed an increasing preference for urban life. About 43 per cent of the 30 million increase
in population in this period was accounted for by immigration. The
shift in immigration from northwestern Europe to southern and
eastern Europe added to the difficulty of absorbing these new
arrivals into the social and industrial life of America and to
the task of labor leaders as they sought to control the labor supply.

The period was one of great industrial growth. The rapid expansion of the western half of the country and the growth in population created steadily growing national markets and a larger labor
supply. Capital was invested in plants and equipment at a mounting
pace, establishments increased in size, and goods and services
were produced to meet a sharply rising demand. The corporate form
of business enterprise, the use of hired management, absentee

ownership, and technological innovations became important features
of our industrial system.

Under these conditions, American wage earners became in-
creasingly interested in labor organizations. Faced with unemployment and loss of income throughout much of the nineties, they
sometimes engaged in violent labor strife which lost them the goodwill of much of the public. With the return of prosperity, they
obtained recognition from employers, negotiated wage contracts, and
grew in membership and influence. Disturbed by the success of the
Federation's organizational drive, a marked increase in strikes
and the growing power of the union movement, many employers joined
together to destroy it. Others continued their dealings with the
union and maintained contractual relations. Still others set out
to develop personnel policies and programs which would make for
more harmonious employee-management relations. The motives of these
employers varied greatly and included the desire to increase
employee efficiency, prevent strikes, reduce unrest, make for
employee loyalty and goodwill, reduce labor turnover and absenteeism, ensure greater social justice, and, not infrequently, to
keep the union out of the organization. It is with the activities
of the third group of employers that this study is concerned.

CHAPTER II

IMPROVEMENT OF PLANT AND WORKING CONDITIONS

The literature of this period does not contain any real evidence that employers had made a concerted effort to improve either
internal or external plant conditions prior to 1890. In fact, the
considerable publicity which accompanied the activities of employers in the period covered by this study testifies to their novelty
at even this late date. Firms which installed even the simplest
improvements, a drinking fountain, for instance, were hailed as
progressive employers.

Many of the innovations of this period are now so completely
integrated into modern management practice that it is indeed difficult to accept the idea that at some point in history they represented departures from customary procedure. In the absence of
social and legislative compulsions, conditions often prevailed
that today would be considered far below the most elementary
standards of safety and sanitation. An experience of the Sherwin-
Williams Company is illustrative of this observation. This company,
a leader in many personnel practices, concluded that a certain
amount of sickness among its employees was due to the drinking
water in the factory. Accordingly, it constructed a device for
filtering drinking water used at the factory.[1] In terms of the

---

1 Tolman, William H., Industrial Betterment (New York: The Social
  Service Press, 1900), p. 8.

22

sanitary standards of the closing decades of the nineteenth century, this action was an innovation.

Landscape Gardening of Factory Grounds

Landscape gardening generally consisted of surrounding the building with a stretch of lawn, dotting it with trees and flowers, and perhaps decorating the buildings with trailing vines.[2] One of the first firms to undertake such a program was the National Cash Register Company of Dayton, Ohio. Describing the efforts of this company, William H. Tolman said:[3]

> The Patterson Brothers in Dayton, Ohio, were led to beautify their factory grounds by the observation of the so-called homes along the line of the railroad. They noted the stiffness and the ugliness of fences, outbuildings, porches and yards, and reflected that much of that same ugliness could be dispelled by the bringing in of beauty. They then decided that their own factory and grounds could be improved....The lawn received their first attention.

In order to accomplish this effort, the company hired a landscape artist. The appearance of the factory was remarkably altered and

---

2 There is a reason to believe that this activity was not too commonly practiced. Mr. Edwin L. Shuey in Factory People and Their Employers (New York: Lentilhon & Co., 1900), p. 36, commented: "Heaps of rubbish, unkept yards and soot-covered buildings unfortunately are the distinguishing mark of many great factories where thousands of men and women are employed. Not only in rolling mills, foundries, and similar iron industries where men only are employed, but also in cotton, woolen, paper and other factories where large numbers of women are busy, do these conditions too often prevail."
3 Tolman, William H., Industrial Betterment, p. 4.

was later used as a model by several other companies.[4] The Roycroft Shop of East Aurora, New York constructed its several buildings in Old English style of architecture in the residential section
of town. These beautiful stone buildings were surrounded by well
kept lawns, shade trees, and flower beds and on one end of the
grounds an orchard and garden were added to improve the beauty of
the plant.[5] The H. J. Heinz Company of Pittsburgh was also a
leader in improving the external appearance of its plant. The
factory was approached through a magnificent portal upon which were
inscribed mottoes designed to inculcate thrift, energy, and content-
ment in the employees, and the grounds around the buildings were
sodded and interspersed with flower beds.[6] The General Electric
Company decorated the main entrance to its Schenectady plant with
beds of flowers, and Boston ivy was planted around the principal
buildings.[7]

The approach of the Magnus Metal Company of Depew, New
York to this problem is described in considerable detail in the
1904 report of the New York State Commissioner of Labor:[8]

> The works are housed in a long and comparably
> narrow two-story brick building. Upon one side
> the outlook is upon a view common to many
> factories located to secure convenient trans-
> portation facilities, viz: a railway siding and

---

4 Shuey, Edwin L., op. cit., p. 43.
5 Stevens, George A., and Hatch, Leonard W., "Employers' Welfare
  Institutions", Third Annual Report of the Commissioner of Labor,
  New York State Department of Labor, (1904), p. 247.
6 Tolman, William H., Industrial Betterment, p. 9.
7 ibid., p. 5.
8 Stevens, George A., and Hatch, Leonard W., op. cit., p. 244.

railroad tracks, but on the other side is a stretch
of lawn nearly a half acre in extent. On that side
also the wall of the factory is over-run with ivy.
The lawn is bordered on the sides next to the street
and the neighboring premises with green hedges,
while on the side next to the factory, a narrow
bed of flowers marks the dividing line between
lawn and ivy. A small one-story tool or supply
house standing in the center of the lawn is robbed
of much of its intrusiveness by similar flower
beds about the base. All this is neatly kept,
and the result of the whole is to give the yard
of a brass foundry an appearance either from
within or without the factory little less attractiveness during the summer months than that of
many a well-appointed private residence.

Other firms which engaged in programs similar to those des-

cribed above were the Eastman Kodak Company, the Natural Food

Company, the New York Central Railroad Repair Shop at Depew, New

York, the Plymouth Cordage Company, Riverside Press at Cambridge,

the Pope Manufacturing Company of Hartford, J. H. McFarland's

Printing House, Harrisburg, Crane's Paper Works at Dalton, the

Bullock Electric Company, and the United States Printing Company

of Cincinnati.[9]

Plant Improvements

Buildings and Internal Appearance

The Plymouth Cordage Company and the Walker and Pratt Manu-

facturing Company were among the early firms which gave consideration

to the needs of their employees in constructing new factory buildings.

---

9 Shuey, Edwin L., op. cit., p. 40.

Of the latter company, William H. Tolman wrote:[10]

> Nearly all the buildings have continuous windows
> with brick walls up to the window sills, thus
> insuring the maximum of light. The area of glass,
> including the warehouse and storage buildings, is
> nearly one quarter the floor area, while in the
> molding shop, partially lighted by skylights, the
> area is thirty-five per cent of the floor area.
> In the molding shop, a large proportion of the
> glass surface is on the north side, thus afford-
> ing a soft and well diffused light and avoiding
> the intense glare of the sunlight.
>   Instead of painting the trusses and structural
> iron work inside the conventional 'foundry red',
> the color is light buff. The roof is painted
> with water paint.

He further states:

> At this same establishment each molder has his
> individual bathing compartment in a room 105 x
> 35 feet. The entire floor is covered with
> concrete, the water draining to a covered
> central gutter. The workman stands on a mov-
> able wooden grating. Each bathing compartment,
> 3 x 5 feet, contains hot and cold water faucets,
> a seat, a pail, and hooks for clothing, while
> a locker fitted with a Yale lock enables the man
> to have his ordinary clothing and valuables in
> security. Overhead incandescent lamps furnish
> light, and steam pipes keep the room comfortably
> warm; white paint has been freely used on all
> the fixtures. One man is in charge of bath and
> washrooms, so that everything is kept neat and
> orderly.

At the Conference on Welfare Work of the National Civic Federation, the following excerpt from a letter written by John Omwake,
President of the U.S. Playing Card Company, was read;[11]

> We built our new factories here with the best
> sanitary conditions we knew how to put in. We

---

10 Tolman, William H., Industrial Betterment, p. 24.
11 National Civic Federation, Proceedings, Conference on Welfare
   Work, (New York: Andrew H. Kellogg Co., 1904), p. 46.

> heat and ventilate the workrooms with a constant
> circulation of fresh air, heated or cooled as the
> occasion requires. We have large, commodious
> dressing rooms, provided with separate lockers
> for each employee. We built a large lunch-room,
> with the best kitchen equipment, where we serve
> the best food at cost only. Music is furnished
> during the lunch hours.

Attention was also directed toward improving the internal
appearance of older plants. The Ferris Brothers of Newark placed
white curtains around the large windows in their plant and then
added potted plants to give it a more home-like appearance.[12]
The National Cash Register Company replaced dingy walls with buff
colored ones and plenty of light, and black machines with buff
colored machinery. Later palms were introduced into the factory.[13]
Another firm, the Barcalo and Boll Manufacturing Company, installed
many conveniences for their employees and provided more attractive
work places by painting the walls and ceilings in two harmonious
shades of green.[14]

Plant Housekeeping

Generally speaking, management did not realize the relation
between good housekeeping practices and safety or cost reduction.
It was the exceptional firm which carried on such activities. One
of these firms, the J. H. Williams Company, was cited with approval
in the Third Annual Report of the New York State Commissioner of

---

12 Tolman, William H., Industrial Betterment, p. 26.
13 ibid., p. 5.
14 Stevens, George A., and Hatch, Leonard W., op. cit., p. 228.

Labor (1904). A portion of this report reads:[15]

> It is a difficult matter to keep an iron works
> absolutely clean, yet the sanitary condition of
> the different workrooms in this factory is as
> nearly perfect as it is possible to make it, and
> this fact is especially noticeable in the machine
> shops, which are light and airy. Dirt is not
> allowed to accumulate on the floors, which are
> subjected to frequent scrubbing. Cuspidors,
> which are furnished to the men by the company,
> are kept reasonably clean. Each employee also
> has a small galvanized iron box attached to the
> wall above his bench, and in this he is obliged
> to deposit all waste.

The economies resulting from efficient housekeeping practices
in the plant were becoming recognized in this period. The manager
of a large iron plant was reported to have saved $3,000 and a new
building by clearing away rubbish and systematically piling his
stock of iron. Another found 7,000 pounds of a valuable product
among a 40,000 pound pile of waste.[16] The following quotation
reveals how little was really being done in this area at the turn
of the century:[17]

> Cleanliness may be obtained by care and attention.
> A few janitors even in a large factory, will keep
> the rooms clean, while the habit of care grows upon
> working people. Waste cans, conveniently placed,
> may not be used at first, but after a while their
> silent invitation is readily accepted. The daily
> emptying of cans and the removal of rubbish and

---

15 ibid., p. 262.
16 Shuey, Edwin L., op. cit., p. 44. The Cleveland Hardware Company found it necessary to prepare a certain part of the factory
for a restaurant they were planning to install. In the process,
they realized that more space was to be gained by keeping everything orderly and cleaned up. The conclusion was then forced
upon the firm that it was money in their pockets to keep the
plant just as clean as possible. (Recounted in Tolman, William H.,
Industrial Betterment, p. 20.)
17 Shuey, Edwin L., op. cit., p. 44.

waste entirely away from the building or to a
special room where it can be disposed of give
assurance of cleanliness and add to available
work room.
Provide a place for all discarded articles,
whether machinery, furniture, supplies or
waste, with proper conditions for disposing
of material not needed, and storage of all
articles that may have future use. All this
is economical, for working people hesitate
to throw away that which may be valuable when
they know it will be seen again the same day.

Ventilation

The first decade of the new century witnessed considerable

public agitation about the social costs of occupational diseases.

It was quite natural, therefore, that attention would be focused

upon undesirable working conditions, and lack of proper ventilation

received its share of criticism. Undoubtedly the few employers

who elected to install some sort of ventilating system were swayed

to a certain extent by this public discussion. Only a handful

of employers, however, attempted to provide ventilation, and these

were frequently neither elaborate nor effective. One of the most

impressive systems was employed by the Natural Food Company and was

described by the company's welfare director before the Conference

on Welfare Work of the National Civic Federation in 1904:[18]

The building is ventilated throughout by the fan
system, the air being changed in the manufacturing
section automatically every fifteen minutes, in
the offices every seven and one-half minutes, and
in the lecture room every five minutes.

---

18 National Civic Federation, Conference on Welfare Work, op. cit.
   p. 151.

> The air is brought in from the tower two hundred
> feet above the ground and is conveyed to the first
> floor of the building, where in the winter it is
> heated and then forced throughout the building.
> Electric thermostats regulate the temperature.

The W. B. Conkey Company also installed an extensive system

of ventilation. In the winter the factory was heated by forcing

fresh air brought from the outside over heated system pipes. In

the summer, the outside air was carried over cooled pipes and then

circulated through the plant.[19] Similar systems were also in use

by the U. S. Playing Card Company, The Hammond Typewriter Com-

pany, the Plymouth Cordage Company, and the Chicago Telephone

Company.[20] The Hammond Typewriter Company had, in addition, a

special refinement: "In the polishing and plating department, which

occupies the top story, there is an improved system of carrying

particles of emery and metal away from the workmen's mouths.

Exhaust fans conduct these minute pieces of matter through pipes

to the roof, where they drop back again into a receptacle and

are thus easily removed from the factory."[21]

Often these facilities were not elaborate as is illustrated

by a description of the system used by the J. H. Williams Company:[22]

---

19 Higinbotham, Harlow N., "How To Secure Employees' Loyalty",
   System, VIII, (July, 1905), 28.
20 Gilman, Nicholas P., A Dividend To Labor, A Study of Employers'
   Welfare Institutions (Boston: Houghton, Mifflin and Company, 1899),
   p. 268.
21 Stevens, George A., and Hatch, Leonard W., op. cit., p. 270.
22 ibid., p. 262.

> Fitted up in the forge room is a unique fresh-air
> cooling apparatus that is a boon to the workmen in
> that department in the hot period of the year. This
> system has tended to greatly improve the general
> health and working qualities of the men. A pipe-
> line, having an outlet over each forge, extends to
> the roof of the building, where blowers force cool
> air through the iron tubing and over the bodies of
> the workers. Before the introduction of this
> device immeasurable discomfort was experienced by
> these employees during the summer months, many of
> them finding it necessary to frequently retire to
> the outer air in order to overcome the effects of
> the heat. Now they are enabled to work without
> any interruption in summer.

Efforts to make work easier and more healthful through proper
ventilating facilities appear to be far from common and most firms
apparently were insufficiently motivated to follow the more progressive leaders.[23]

Illumination

With the exception of a few firms, including the Walker and
Pratt Manufacturing Company and the U. S. Playing Card Company,
this aspect of working conditions appears to have received a
minimum of attention. Evidence which indicates that illumination
had received less attention than ventilation appeared in the
American Labor Legislation Review in 1911. Writing on this

---

23 Even as late as 1920, ventilating facilities were far from
   adequate. "Needless to say such conditions -- 68 degrees
   temperature, with not more than 65 relative humidity -- are
   rarely obtained in factory rooms. Of 215 workrooms in New
   York State recently investigated, nearly one third had a
   temperature of 80 degrees or over and three fourths of 73
   degrees or over." Taken from Frankel, Lee K., and Fleischer,
   Alexander, The Human Factor in Industry (New York: The
   Macmillan Company, 1920), p. 159.

subject, E. Leavenworth Elliott said: "The relation of light and illumination to the health and efficiency of the factory worker has received less attention in proportion to its importance than that of any other single facility or condition. There are only eleven states that make any mention of the subject of light in their general factory or labor laws, and in not one of these are the provisions sufficiently specific to render them of practical value."[24] In an investigation in 1912, the New York State Factory Commission reported that 36.7 per cent of the laundries investigated, 49.2 per cent of the candy factories, 50 per cent of the ice-cream plants, and 64.8 per cent of the chemical establishments were inadequately lighted.[25] An indication that employers were not cognizant of the relationship between proper lighting and increased productivity is confirmed by an article on lighting written in 1911:[26]

> Besides being entirely practical, these provisions
> would in no wise be burdensome to the manufacturer;
> on the contrary, they would be highly beneficial.
> Good and sufficient lighting is, generally speaking,
> cheaper than bad and insufficient lighting; it is
> simply a question of the proper selection and use
> of the numerous forms of lamps and accessories now
> available. But of far greater importance than the
> cost of light is the increase in output which
> results from good and sufficient illumination. It
> can easily be shown that a good workman earning
> only $2.00 per day of ten hours would have to

---

24 Elliott, E. Leavenworth, "Factory Lighting", American Labor
   Legislation Review, I, No. 2, (June, 1911), 113.
25 Frankel, Lee K., and Fleischer, Alexander, op. cit., p. 155.
26 Elliott, E. Leavenworth, op. cit., p. 116.

lose but three minutes of his time to make a loss
to the manufacturer equal to the cost of all the
artificial light he could possibly require during
the entire day.

Fire Prevention

Activities for fire prevention and control, although not
uniformly or universally practiced, found favor with some companies.
In certain states, legislation forced employers to provide measures
for fire control, particularly after several disastrous fires
demonstrated how costly inadequate fire protection could be.[27]
Among the firms in the forefront was the Acme Lead and Color Works
of Detroit, whose fire department was organized in 1900. The
company maintained a regular fire department and, in addition,
organized a volunteer group of fire fighters in each department.
An automatic sprinkler was installed for every eight square feet
and drills were held regularly to keep the employees alert and
trained.[28] The Westinghouse Electric and Manufacturing Company
not only fully equipped its plant with an automatic sprinkler

---

27 Not all states had adequate legislation with respect to fire
prevention. However, the New Jersey law had detailed rules
for the prevention of fire and for means of escape in case of
fire. Ohio, Wisconsin, Minnesota, Colorado, and New Hampshire
required certain standards of fire safety and Pennsylvania
provided for fire drills in all industrial establishments where
women or girls were employed.

28 Tolman, William H., Social Engineering (New York: McGraw-Hill
Book Co., 1909), p. 106. Among the other firms which provided
similar protection about this same time were the Parke, Davis
and Company; the Curtis Publishing Company which issued a
special booklet of instructions to employees on fire prevention;
the Westinghouse Electric and Manufacturing Company; the Waltham
Watch Company; the Strawbridge and Clothier Department Store;
the Baldwin Locomotive Works; Broadway Department Store in Los
Angeles; and the Lynchburg Cotton Mills.

system, fire walls and doors of fire resisting material but also organized a fire department of eight companies of ten men each.[29] The Baldwin Locomotive Works designed its elaborate fire protection system in accordance with its insurance contract with the Factory Mutual Fire Insurance Company. Seven fire pumps were maintained, six of which were located in the main part of the works. Each building was equipped with automatic sprinklers. Water tanks were situated on the top of stair and elevator towers and water was directed to specific points by an elaborate system of pipes and controls.[30]

Sanitary Facilities

During the two decades under consideration, some employers inaugurated programs aimed at the improvement of sanitary facilities for employees. Shower baths and private locker rooms with basins for washing were distinct innovations of this period. These facilities were made available during and immediately after work and in many cases employees used them in lieu of proper sanitary facilities at home. Drinking fountains and more decent toilet conditions were concomitant innovations.

Bathing and Wash Room Facilities

In 1893 the J. H. Williams and Company of Brooklyn, estab-

---

29 ibid., p. 109.
30 ibid., p. 110.

lished the first baths for employees in an industrial plant.[31]
These baths were placed in rooms that also contained lockers and
were for the use of the employees after work and also on Saturday.
Shortly thereafter, the Sherwin-Williams Paint Company and the
Ferris Brothers also added baths in their establishments.[32] The
Hygienic Chemical Company of Elizabethport, New Jersey, about this
same time, instituted bathing facilities for employees and furnished
soap and towels free. In this establishment, every employee was
allowed twenty minutes once a week during working hours for
bathing purposes without deduction of wages. During the summer
months, this was increased to two twenty-minute periods per week.
However, no restriction was placed on the number of baths that could
be taken after working hours.[33]

Some of these bathing rooms were quite ornate as is evident
from the following description given by E. F. Olmstead, in charge
of welfare work for the Natural Food Company:[34]

> The bathing facilities of the conservatory are
> probably equalled by few hotels in the country.
> There are fourteen rooms devoted to baths, each
> room being finished in Italian marble and mosaic.
> The men's rooms are equipped with shower and
> needle baths and the girls' rooms with individual
> bathtubs and ring showers.

---

31 Tolman, William H., Social Engineering, p. 67.
32 ibid., p. 66.
33 ibid., p. 68. The National Cash Register Company also used the
   system of one bath a week on company time in the winter and two
   in the summer.
34 National Civic Federation, Conference on Welfare Work, op. cit.,
   p. 155. William H. Tolman, in Industrial Betterment, p. 24, estimated that these bathing facilities were provided by the company
   at a cost of approximately $100,000.

> The employees are allowed ample time each week
> for the use of these baths. Soap and towels are
> free.
> This feature of our work has been very successful...
> Its use is entirely at their own discretion, and all
> that is necessary is for them to ask permission of
> the forewoman or foreman, so that others may be
> assigned to their places in order that the work may
> not be interrupted. The time used for this purpose
> averages about one hour per week per person.

Although it was obviously necessary for firms in the food

processing industries to be interested in securing cleanliness,

the furnishing of bathing facilities was not confined to this type

of industry. The J. H. Williams Company, for example, furnished

very extensive facilities:[35]

> ...in addition to spray baths for their employees,
> (the company has) a wash trough fitted up with
> small douche baths so that the men can thoroughly
> wash their hands after the day's work. Another
> large trough is provided with a wringer so that
> the men can quickly wash their underclothes which
> are usually soaked with perspiration and dirt. A
> drying closet is provided with hot water pipes so
> that the clothes can be dried and when the men
> come the next morning they have a clean, sweet
> suit in which to begin the day's work.

Bathing facilities in some firms were closely linked to the

prevention of occupational diseases. Many of the paint companies

were especially concerned with the harmful effects of lead. As a

result, they installed baths and furnished other sanitary facilities.[36]

---

35 Shuey, Edwin L., op. cit., p. 51-2.
36 Jones, Edward D., The Administration of Industrial Enterprises
   (New York: Longmans, Green and Company, 1920), p. 296. Among
   other firms which had installed bathing facilities during this
   period were the Walker and Pratt Manufacturing Company whose
   facilities were quite elaborate; the Plymouth Cordage Company;

Companies found that these conveniences for employees were a factor in attracting better employees.[37]

Lockers

As a general rule, lockers for changing clothes and storing valuables were furnished in conjunction with bathing facilities. In the fall of 1902, the Barcalo and Boll Manufacturing Company of Buffalo included individual, ventilated lockers in its general improvement program provided for its female employees.[38] The H. J. Heinz Company supplied its female employees with neat blue gowns and white caps and then provided a dressing room with an individual locker for each girl.[39] The Cleveland Cliffs Iron Company built a new "changing house" containing shower baths, wash basins, racks for drying mine clothes and lockers for the men.[40] The New York

---

The Cleveland Cliffs Iron Company; the National Lead Company; the Sherwin-Williams Paint Company; the Colorado Fuel and Iron Company; the Weston Electrical Instrument Company; the Ayers Machine Company; the United Shoe Machinery Company; the Pope Manufacturing Company, and the S.E. Packard and Sons Company.

37 The President of the Enterprise Manufacturing Company of Philadelphia, after he had introduced baths for his moulders, testified: "I wish to impress upon you the importance of a bath room for moulders in every foundry in the country. If you can contribute in any way to this end you certainly will be doing much good. A warm shower bath, together with putting on dry, clean clothes, is worth a very great deal to a moulder, and we find that we have the pick of men. They are very anxious to work for us in preference to other foundries." Related in Shuey, Edwin L., op. cit., p. 51.

38 Stevens, George A., and Hatch, Leonard W., op. cit., p. 227.

39 Tolman, William H., Industrial Betterment, p. 69.

40 National Civic Federation, Conference on Welfare Work, op. cit., p. 158.

Telephone Company provided wire lockers for the storage of the girls' hats and coats with keys that were kept by a matron.[41]

Drinking Water Facilities

In addition to the Sherwin-Williams Company, there were other firms who exhibited interest in the problem of sanitary drinking facilities.[42] The general motivation toward the provision of satisfactory drinking water is revealed in the report of the New York State Commissioner of Labor in 1904:[43]

> Considerable working in lead is necessary in the manufacture of the National Battery Company's product, and unless some preventive is used, the lead fumes tend to produce 'lead colic.' For this reason, the firm supplies its employees with medicated drinking water in the various workrooms, the use of which is an effective preventive of the disease.

In both of the instances cited, the firms were operating under unusual conditions and good drinking water was a real problem. The Natural Food Company also provided sterilized water and, in addition, furnished drinking glasses for the employees.[44]

Ice water was sometimes furnished in the summer months, although it was not universally practiced. Edwin L. Shuey

---

41 Gilman, Nicholas P., op. cit., p. 269. The United States Playing Card Company, the Pope Manufacturing Company, the J. H. Williams Company, the New York Couch Bed Company, the New York Bread Company, the L. A. Cushman Company, and the Fest Biscuit Company of New York were among other firms which furnished locker and wardrobe facilities.
42 Tolman, William H., Industrial Betterment, p. 17.
43 Stevens, George A., and Hatch, Leonard W., op. cit., p. 238.
44 National Civic Federation, Conference on Welfare Work, op. cit., p. 158.

reported:[45]

> Another seemingly very small matter has proved,
> wherever tried, to be one of great value. It
> seems a very small thing to furnish ice water
> during the summer or the entire year for men who
> must work in warm rooms. In hundreds of establish-
> ments in this country, the men contribute among
> themselves for this purpose. The Enterprise
> Manufacturing Company and others furnish the ice
> water in good, clean receptacles and have a man
> whose duty it is to see that these are properly
> attended to.

Provisions for Rest

Rest Rooms

The importance of rest periods during the day was recognized
and a number of companies provided clean, comfortable rest rooms
for their employees. Writing in 1900, Edwin L. Shuey said: "The
provision of a rest room, which has come to be regarded as important in many factories, especially where women are employed, is
valuable just as truly for men in factories where work is very
heavy or hazardous."[46] Among the firms which provided a rather
elaborate rest room was the Barcalo and Boll Manufacturing Company
whose activity was described in the Third Annual Report of the
New York State Commissioner of Labor:[47]

> The rest room, which is about 15 feet square, is
> furnished with a view to both comfort and attrac-
> tiveness. Papered walls and ceiling, rug for the
> floor, center table, easy chairs and couch combined,

45 Shuey, Edwin L., op. cit., p. 55.
46 ibid., p. 48.
47 Stevens, George A., and Hatch, Leonard W., op. cit., p. 227.

> produce a home-like appearance in pleasing contrast
> to the nearby work rooms. Ferns and palms, and in
> the summer time, flowering plants in a window box,
> give further cheerfulness to the place, and di-
> version as well as rest is offered by the files of
> two magazines received regularly at the room.

The rest or lounging rooms were also available in the event of

sickness or accident.

Rest Periods

Rest periods during the day, especially for female employees,

were permitted by some companies. Twice a day, the employees of

the New York Telephone Company could leave their seats for twenty

minutes' rest from their work.[48] The women of the Chicago Tele-

phone Company had the benefit of a relief system which protected

them against undue strain.[49] The girls of the Natural Food

Company were granted fifteen minutes every morning and afternoon

for rest and recreation,[50] and about 1900, a large Chicago office

introduced the custom of serving tea and wafers to its force of

young women stenographers at three o'clock each afternoon.[51] A

few firms used these rest periods in the day to provide exercises

for their employees. The description of this practice in the

Kinnard Manufacturing Company of Dayton, Ohio is of interest:[52]

48 Gilman, Nicholas P., op. cit., p. 269.
49 ibid., p. 268.
50 National Civic Federation,Conference on Welfare Work, op. cit.
   p. 157.
51 Shuey, Edwin L., op. cit., p. 75.
52 Olmstead, Victor H., "The Betterment of Industrial Conditions",
   U. S. Department of Commerce and Labor, Bulletin No. 31,(Washington:
   Government Printing Office, 1900), p. 1133. The Roycroft Shop
   also had a 15 minute period daily where girls could voluntarily
   participate in gymnastics under the guidance of the company
   physical director.

President Kinnard, of this company, which is a
large manufacturing concern of Dayton with many
female employees states that during the summer
of 1898 considerable trouble was encountered
because of the fact that the experienced force
of the establishment was constantly being
depleted on account of sudden illness and
fainting spells among the women, as many as
seven or eight a day being frequently compelled
to quit work. Physicians were summoned to
examine the factory and its management for the
purpose of ascertaining the cause of these
frequent collapses, and they all pronounced
the sanitary conditions to be perfect. No
cause for the excessive rate of sickness could
be found, and it was finally suggested that
perhaps the trouble was caused by too close
application on the part of the women to their
work, and that a little rest in the forenoons
and afternoons would probably be found beneficial. The suggestion was promptly acted upon,
and an informal calisthenics club was immediately
formed, a competent instructor employed by the
company, and ever since the female employees
have been given 15 minutes' recess each morning
and afternoon, during which all the women join in
light gymnastic exercises.

Miscellaneous Improvements in Working Conditions

Improvements in the Workplace

Although the principles of scientific management were
initially enunciated during the period under consideration, they
were infrequently, if at all, applied by employers. This is
apparent from the attitude of indifference which was manifested
toward improvements in the workplace to increase productivity.
In 1904, Edwin L. Shuey reported:[53]

In foundries and machine rooms where small work
is done, employes sit during the entire day. It
seems not to have occurred to many employers

---

53 Shuey, Edwin L., op. cit., p. 55.

that backs to these chairs and foot stools would
not only give comfort to the employe, but would
add to his productivity ability. An experiment
in this direction has proved that 25 per cent
to 50 per cent of increase may be noted in the
output resulting from the bracing of the back
and the comfortable position in which the
operatives work; at the same time the employe
is able to work throughout the day with very
little fatigue.

This general deficiency was also noted by another writer who des-

cribed conditions in the canning industry:[54]

The fatigue of the work at the conveyors or
sorting tables is increased by the unnecessarily
constrained and uncomfortable positions to which
the girls are subjected. The tables are rarely
at a right height to make this work as easy as
possible. Sometimes they are so high that the
workers must stand all day; sometimes so low
(3 feet from the ground) that the workers cannot
sit with their knees under the tables, but work
in twisted and awkward attitudes. Moreover, the
seats themselves are totally inadequate. According to the New York report, of about 1,400 girls
and women engaged in sorting peas and beans at
various factories in the summer of 1908, only
about 180 had chairs to sit upon. The others
were supplied with inadequate boxes, crates, and
stools, or benches.

Several firms, however, including the National Cash Register

Company and the Natural Food Company had taken the initiative by

1910 in supplying their female employees with chairs with comfort-

able backs and footstools.[55]

Uniforms and Laundry Service

The S. E. Packard and Sons Company of Campello, Massa-

---

54 Goldmark, Josephine, Fatigue and Efficiency (New York: Survey
   Associates, Inc., 1912), p. 61-2.
55 Gilman, Nicholas P., op. cit., p. 268.

chusetts, provided uniform overalls and coats for the men and
laundered them at the company's expense.[56] New employees at
the Patton Paint Company were furnished at the outset of their
employment with two suits of overalls. Originally the company
sent them to a private laundry and the cost was shared equally
by the company and the men. Finding this to be too expensive
and inconvenient, the company finally installed laundry facilities and furnished this service free to the men.[57] Other
companies which supplied certain items of apparel free, were
the Brooklyn Bridge Railway Company, the National Cash Register
Company, the Barcalo and Boll Manufacturing Company, the Sherwin-
Williams Paint Company, the H. J. Heinz and Company, and the F. A.
Brownell Company of Rochester.

Conclusion

Many improvements in the plant and in working conditions
which were begun by a few progressive employers in the early
years of this period gathered momentum after the turn of the
century. In discussing the activities of the members of the
Industrial Committee of the Cleveland Chamber of Commerce,
William H. Tolman said:[58]

> The most gratifying progress is evidenced in
> the general inclination of employers towards
> the provision of light, well ventilated,

---

56 ibid., p. 70.
57 National Civic Federation, Conference on Welfare Work, op. cit.,
   p. 55.
58 Tolman, William H., Industrial Betterment, p. 46.

comfortable and wholesome stores and factories,
and of other means for securing the health and
comfort of employees -- features which were
originally considered extraneous to business
and classed as distinctive betterment work,
but which are now provided as a matter of course.
    Hardly a factory is now built without provision
for rest, recreation and lunch rooms, and the
general tendency toward improvement is shown in
the fact that the building code recently adopted
by the city lays especial emphasis upon sufficient
light, air and toilet facilities.

It is always difficult to assess the motives which lead

employers to make innovations. The literature does not throw

much light on employer motivation with respect to these personnel

activities. Undoubtedly, certain employers voluntarily sought

to make the work environment more pleasant and to provide greater

comfort to their employees. Some of them, as for example the

paint manufacturers and the producers of storage batteries, were

concerned with the health of their workers. Others were prompted

to take action because of the growing public concern over indus-

trial accidents and occupational diseases. Some states and cities

passed laws or ordinances requiring the maintenance of minimum

standards in business establishments but these, in the main, did

not apply to industrial accidents or occupational diseases.

Many employers found that such activities not only made

for more comfortable working conditions and more pleasant

surroundings but improved employee morale, increased productivity,

attracted better workmen to the plant, and, as a result, reduced production costs.

That progressive employers did not always have a free hand in undertaking such activities but had to convince their stockholders that such improvement should be made is indicated by the testimony of an executive of the Weston Electrical Instrument Company at the National Civic Federation's Conference on Welfare Work in 1904 as reported by William H. Tolman:[59]

> Invariably in questioning why such conditions (unsatisfactory working conditions) exist the answer is 'It doesn't pay to make better accommodations because the men abuse them.' That this is not always the case finds illustration at the works of the Weston Electrical Instrument Company. ...When the works were planned, some of the directors doubted the wisdom of so expensive a system; they feared the motive might not be appreciated or the property respected, and cited the fact that the water closets in the old works had met the customary fate. The president replied that in the old establishment there had been nothing to appeal to the personal self-respect of the men, or their respect for the property, and that he believed the proposed new departure would be received with favor by the employees; 'Anyway,' said he, 'I am going to investigate this question myself' and he did. He went into all sections of New York City, from Carnegie Hall to the slums; and his report was that wherever he found superior water closets he found them respected.

---

59 Tolman, William H., Social Engineering, p. 6.

CHAPTER III

DINING FACILITIES

The examination of dining facilities furnished by employers
in this twenty-year period will be concerned not only with restaurants in which meals were served, but also with lunch rooms set
aside by employers in which employees could eat their own lunches
away from their work place. The establishment of dining facilities
for employees seems to have been more popular with employers than
many other personnel activities which were carried on during this
period.

Origin of Several Dining Programs

There is not a great deal of information available on the
reasons which prompted employers to introduce dining programs.
Existing evidence does indicate, however, that often their in-
ception grew out of the needs of the employees. No particular
pattern is discernible. The Acme White Lead and Color Works
started to furnish food, for instance, after making a careful
study of the eating habits of their employees. They discovered
that some of the workers left home without breakfast or did not
eat much at noon. The Company felt that it would be desirable
for these employees to get wholesome food, even during working
hours, and so, restaurant facilities, were established.[1] The

---

1 Tolman, William H., Social Engineering (New York: McGraw-Hill
  Book Company, 1909), p. 82. The Lisk Manufacturing Company of

management of the Cleveland Hardware Company, Canton, Ohio
observed that many of the men came away from home without breakfast and spent part of their working time in eating. The company,
unable to curtail this practice, decided that a restaurant might
solve the problem. Provision was made for the employees to get
food at a specified time in the morning and at the noon hour.[2]

In the case of the Gorham Manufacturing Company of Providence, Rhode Island, the president decided that, since most of the
employees lived a considerable distance from the plant, it would
be more pleasant for them to eat their cold lunches in some nice,
airy, comfortable place rather than at their work benches. Such
a place was provided, but shortly after, the president decided
that a hot dinner would be much more beneficial to his employees
and started a restaurant.[3]

How the restaurant of the National Cash Register Company of
Dayton, Ohio was established has been told by William H. Tolman:[4]

New York, according to the New York State Commissioner of Labor,
had this same problem of light breakfasts by employees. This
company, however, made arrangements for a dairyman to enter the
factory daily between 9:00 and 11:00 o'clock to sell milk at
$0.05 per quart. It was estimated that 75% of the employees
availed themselves of this service.

2 Tolman, William H., Industrial Betterment (New York: The Social
Service Press, 1900), p. 22.
3 ibid., p. 19.
4 ibid., p. 18. The dining facilities of the Tanner's Shoe Stock
Company, Olean, New York, were started in the same manner. The
habit of warming tea or coffee in bottles upon the steam pipes
in the work rooms, with the frequent result of broken bottles
from overheating suggested to the company's manager, the provision of better means for supplying hot drinks. In 1901 a

One day Mr. J. H. Patterson, President of the National Cash Register Company, passing through his factory about twenty minutes to twelve o'clock, observed a girl leave her work bench with a pail, which she put on the radiator. Calling the forewoman he asked why the girl warmed the glue on the radiator and not in the usual place. 'Glue?' said the forewoman, 'that isn't glue, that's coffee.' On learning this fact he was impressed in the first instance by the loss of time to him, caused by the girl leaving her work bench twenty minutes before twelve o'clock; and secondly, he said to himself that it must be a pretty poor apology for coffee if it was saved over from breakfast and warmed up on a radiator. On reflection he decided that it would be a saving to him of time and money, as well as beneficial to the girls, for him to provide hot coffee at the company's expense. This experiment gave so much mutual satisfaction that he next made a few dietary sutdies of the kind of food which the girls brought and the way in which it was prepared. He found in many instances that there was not enough food and that it was of poor quality. Frequently the food was spoiled in the cooking. Continuing his reflection, he observed to himself, 'If my operatives have insufficient or poorly cooked food they are not able to do a full days work.' Then he decided that it would be a saving of money for the company to provide a warm mid-day meal. An attic in the factory which had served as a kind of store room was cleaned out, large windows put in, and the room freshly painted in cheery colors and fitted up with small circular tables. Now the girls had a dining room flooded with sunshine and good cheer, where a meal consisting of soup, meat, one vegetable, plenty of bread and butter, tea or coffee, and one dessert is provided at the expense of the company. The girls take turns in waiting on each other. The expense to the company of the dinner, exclusive of the preparation of the food, is about 4½ cents a day for each individual. Mr. Patterson states that under no circumstances would he return to the old conditions, being convinced that the expense of providing sufficient, well-cooked food under hygenic conditions and surroundings has been more than offset by the increased amount of work in the department where the girls are employed.

---

small room was partitioned off the main work room and facilities were installed at a cost of $28.00.

Nature of Dining Facilities

Table I presents the dining facilities of forty companies.
The table gives the name of the company, the nature of the
business, the number of employees, and the eating facilities
provided. Information as to when these companies first installed
these facilities is not available. However, a survey of dining
facilities reported in the Third Annual Report of the Commissioner
of Labor of New York State in 1904, stated that of twenty companies
studied, only one company, the New York Quinine and Chemical Works,
initiated its dining facilities prior to 1890; three companies
started this activity in the period 1890-94; four in the period
1895-99 and twelve between 1900 and 1904, inclusive.[5]

An examination of the geographical location of these forty
companies shows a significant concentration in New England and in
the Middle Atlantic states. Twenty-six companies, about 60%,
were located in the northeastern area of the country. The mid-
western states, including Ohio, accounted for eleven firms.
Only one firm was located in the South and two were located in the
far West.

It will be observed that dining facilities were not peculiar to

---

5 Stevens, George A., and Hatch, Leonard W., "Employers' Welfare
  Institutions", Third Annual Report of the Commissioner of Labor,
  New York State Department of Labor, (1904), pp. 225-329. From
  the context of the material in the major sources used to compile
  Table I, the writer is of the opinion that very few companies
  furnished this facility prior to 1890.

Table I
Dining Facilities and Lunch Rooms[1]

Company and Location	Business	Number of Employees	Nature of Facilities
Acme White Lead and Color Works, Detroit, Mich.	Paints	500	Lunch room; free coffee
American Locomotive Company, Schenectady and Dunkirk, N.Y.	Steel Fabricator	n.a.	Meals at low prices
Atchison, Topeka and Santa Fe Railroad	Railroad	n.a.	Reduced prices at company restaurants
Carter, Howe and Company, Newark, N. J.	Manufacturer, Jewelry	325	Lunch rooms; no meals; kitchen facilities
Cleveland Axle Company, Canton, O.	Manufacturer, Axles	200	Meals paid for by employees
Cleveland Hardware Company, Cleveland, Ohio	Manufacturer, Hardware	1,200	Meals at low prices; later a lunch room
Curtis Publishing Company, Philadelphia, Pa.	Publisher	1,000	Meals with a suggestion system for improvements
Eastern and Western Lumber Company, Portland, Ore.	Manufacturer, Lumber	700	Lunch room; free coffee and soup
Ferris Brothers, Newark, New Jersey	Manufacturer, Corsets and Waists	400	Lunch room with tea and coffee furnished free
General Electric Company, Schenectady, N. Y.	Manufacturer, Electrical equipment	n.a.	Meals furnished at fixed prices
Gorham Manufacturing Company, Providence, R. I.	Silver and Goldsmiths	1,900	Meals at low prices
Hale Brothers, San Francisco, Calif.	Department Store	800	Lunch room with stove
Heinz Manufacturing Company, Pittsburgh, Pa.	Food Processor	4,345	Lunch room; coffee fund started by employees
International Harvester Company	Farm Machinery	30,000	Meals at low prices at several plants
Iron Clad Manufacturing Company, Brooklyn, N. Y.	Steel Fabricator	1,500	Meals at low prices

Table I (continued)

Company and Location	Business	Number of Employees	Nature of Facilities
James R. Keiser Company, New York City	Manufacturer, ties & Belts	400	Lunch room; stove and refrigerator furnished
Ludlow Manufacturing Company, Ludlow, Mass.	Jute & Hemp	3,000	Meals at low prices
Lynchburg Cotton Mill, Lynchburg, Virginia	Cotton Mill	550	Lunch room
Maddock Pottery Company, Trenton, N.J.	Pottery	250	Meals at low prices
Metropolitan Life Insurance Company, New York City	Insurance	14,000	Meals at low prices
Milford Shoe Company, Milford, Mass.	Manufacturer, Men's shoes	385	Meals at cost; profits went to benefit fund
National Biscuit Company, New York City	Biscuits and Crackers	2,000	Meals at cost
National Cash Register Company, Dayton, Ohio	Manufacturer, Cash Registers	3,785	Meals served free
Natural Food Company, Niagara Falls, N. Y.	Wheat Products	400	Meals served free to girls; at low prices to men
New York Telephone Company, New York, N. Y.	Telephone Company	n.a.	Lunch room; tea, coffee and chocolate free
Patton Paint Company, Milwaukee, Wis.	Manufacturer, Paint	350	Lunch room; free kitchen facilities
George B. Peck Dry Goods Company, Kansas City, Mo.	Dry Goods Store	900	Meals served at low prices
Plymouth Cordage Company, Plymouth, Mass.	Manufacturers, Cordage	1,220	Meals served at low prices
Pope Manufacturing Company, Hartford, Conn.	Manufacturer, Bicycles	1,000	Meals served at low prices
Sherwin-Williams Paint Company, Cleveland, Ohio	Manufacturer, Paint and Varnish	2,000	Lunch room; special items at low prices
Solvay Process Company, Solvay, N.Y.	Alkalies	2,500	Meals served at low prices

Table I (continued)

Company and Location	Business	Number of Employees	Nature of Facilities
Strawbridge & Clothier, Philadelphia, Pa.	Department Store	5,500	Lunch room; coffee, tea furnished free
Tide Water Oil Company, Bayonne, N. J.	Petroleum Refining	1,200	Lunch room with free facilities and utensils
U. S. Playing Card Company, Cincinnati, Ohio	Manufacturer, Playing cards	n.a.	Lunch room; meals furnished at cost
Waltham Watch Company, Waltham, Mass.	Manufacturer, Watches	4,131	Meals furnished at cost; lunch room too
John Wanamaker, Philadelphia, Pa.	Department Store	n.a.	Meals furnished at low prices
Warner Brothers, Bridgeport, Conn.	Manufacturer, Corsets	n.a.	Meals at low prices
Wayne Knitting Mills, Fort Wayne, Ind.	Manufacturer, Hosiery	1,500	Meals at low prices
Weston Electrical Instrument Company, Newark, N. J.	Electrical Instruments	368	Meals served at low prices
Westinghouse Electric & Manufacturing, Pittsburgh, Pa.	Electrical apparatus	17,000	Meals at low prices; lunch room

n.a. Not available

1 This table has been compiled from the following sources: Gilman, Nicholas P., A Dividend to Labor, A Study of Employers' Welfare Institutions (Boston: Houghton, Mifflin and Company, 1899) 400 pp.; National Civic Federation, Proceedings, Conference on Welfare Work (New York: Andrew H. Kellogg Co., 1904), 199 pp.; Tolman, William H., Industrial Betterment, 1900; and Tolman, William H., Social Engineering, 1909.

firms of any particular size. Nine of the companies had less than
500 employees; five firms had between 500 and 999 employees; fifteen firms had between 1,000 and 4,999 employees, and only four
of the firms had 5,000 or more employees.

Table I also reveals the type of dining facilities which the
various firms had. Twenty-three of the firms furnished meals,
usually at very low prices, and seventeen firms maintained lunch
rooms to which employees could bring their luncheons.[6] Many of
those companies which furnished only lunch rooms, however, supplied
free coffee and tea to the employees. In some cases, a stove and
other kitchen facilities were supplied so that hot meals could be
prepared. Only two of these firms, The National Cash Register
Company and the Natural Food Company, furnished meals free of
charge to their employees.[7] All other firms charged for meals,
although in some cases, the prices were set just high enough to
cover costs. On this matter, Edwin L. Shuey reported:[8]

---

6 "The most popular form of employee's restaurant was the self-
  service cafeteria. Variety of food was combined with cheapness
  by reducing the amount of service furnished." See Frankel,
  Lee K., and Fleischer, Alexander, The Human Factor in Industry
  (New York: The Macmillan Company, 1920), p. 228.
7 The Sherwin-Williams Paint Company, in addition to furnishing
  free tea and coffee daily, also served one hot dish free to
  employees. The free courses included: Monday, beef stew; Tues-
  day, barley soup; Wednesday, baked beans; Thursday, vegetable
  soup; Friday, oysters, fish or chowder; Saturday, pea soup.
  Charges, however, were made for extras.
8 Shuey, Edwin L., Factory People and Their Employers (New York:
  Lentilhon and Co., 1900), p. 76.

> The usual custom is to make the charges only such
> as will cover the cost of supplying the lunch it-
> self. In most of these instances, instead of pay-
> ing for the meals in cash, the men pay for them
> in meal tickets which are provided by the company
> and which may be bought in sums of 25¢, 50¢, and
> $1.

In order to give an indication of the type of food and the prices that were charged at the beginning of the century, the menu of the dining hall of the Dunkirk plant of the American Locomotive Company is presented.

It should be pointed out that the menu of the American Locomotive Company was more elaborate than that of many companies, but the prices charged were fairly typical. Of ten companies which disclosed their prices, eight charged between ten and fifteen cents.[9] These included the Ludlow Manufacturing Company, the National Cash Register Company, and John Wanamaker Philadelphia, all of whom charged fifteen cents; the Plymouth Cordage Company and the Cleveland Hardware Company which charged twelve cents, and the Acme White Lead Company, the Natural Food Company, and the American Locomotive Company which charged ten cents. The Tide Water Oil Company charged only five cents for

---

9 Five companies in Rochester, New York, which were not included in the above group of firms, also charged fifteen cents per meal. When an employer asked Mrs. Hotchkiss, the supervisor of res- taurants, to serve a fifteen-cent lunch, she said she could not undertake a lunch for one hundred people for less than sixteen cents a head except at a loss. She finally agreed to try and the experiment proved to be a huge success with the number of employees served increasing from 100 to 400. Lattimore, Alida, "Quick Lunches for Efficiency and Health," Survey, XXV (March, 1911), p. 1013.

Menu at the Dining Hall of the Dunkirk Plant of the
American Locomotive Company[10]

Dinner

Chowders	3¢	Salads	3¢
Vegetable Soup	3¢	Tomatoes	3¢
Vermicelli Soup	3¢	Boiled Onions	3¢
Split Pea Soup	3¢	Beets	3¢
Tomato Soup	3¢	Boiled Cabbage	3¢
Queen Olives	3¢	Pies (all kinds) per slice	3¢
Lamb and Beef Stews	3¢	Custards	3¢
Roast Pork & Applesauce	3¢	Plum pudding with hardsauce	3¢
Roast prime beef & Dish		Jellies	3¢
Gravy	3¢	Cakes	3¢
Spring Lamb and mint		Domestic Cheese	3¢
Sauce	3¢	Swiss Cheese	3¢
Cold Ham	3¢	Fruit	1&2¢
Pickled Pigs' Feet	3¢	Coffee	3¢
Mutton	3¢	Milk	3¢
Mashed Potatoes	3¢	Horseradish........)	
Sweet Potatoes	3¢	Pepper Sauce.......)	
Turnips	3¢	Worchestershire Sauce.) Free	
Peas	3¢	Table Sauce.........)	
Corn	3¢	Catsup..............)	

Breakfast and Supper

Fruit in Season	3¢	Coffee	3¢
Milk	3¢	Tea	3¢
Chocolate	3¢	Oatmeal	3¢
Force	3¢	Shredded Wheat Biscuit	3¢
Codfish Balls	3¢	**Eggs (One)**	
Sandwiches		Boiled	3¢
Ham	3¢	Scrambled	3¢
Chicken	3¢	Fried, 3¢ poached on toast	3¢
Domestic Cheese	3¢	Boston Baked Beans	3¢
Swiss Cheese	3¢	Potato Salad	3¢
Egg	3¢	**Potatoes**	
Oyster	3¢	French Fried	3¢
Small Steak, potatoes,		Hashed Brown	3¢
bread and butter	3¢	Baked	3¢
Sugar Cured Ham	3¢	**Bread**	
Chops	3¢	Pullman loaf, Boston brown	3¢
Liver and Onions	3¢	Rye, Corn Cakes	3¢
Hamburg Steak	3¢	Buckwheat Cakes	3¢
Bacon	3¢	Syrup and Butter	3¢
Fried oysters, two for	3¢	Buttered Toast	3¢
Hot frankfurters, two for	3¢	Waffles	3¢
Porterhouse Steak	15¢	Bread or rolls with butter	3¢

10 Reprinted from National Civic Federation, Conference on Welfare Work,

its meals, whereas the General Electric Company, under its
arrangement with a private restauranteur, charged twenty cents
for meals.[11]

The actual physical facilities provided by employers, as was
to be expected, differed greatly. Frankel and Fleischer wrote:[12]

> The arrangements made for providing hot lunches for
> employees were many and varied - from the gas jet
> in a dark corner of the workshop over which an im-
> provised iron ring held the coffee pot while up-
> turned boxes served as tables and chairs, to the
> chintz decorated dining room with small tables and
> service. The type and amount of accommodation
> provided depended upon the distance of the factory
> from the homes of the workers, the kind of workers
> served, and the number and quality of neighboring
> restaurants.

The H. J. Heinz Company provided a special dining room
which was decorated with pictures and plants and had accommodations for 500 girls who brought their lunches. Each girl
paid a penny a day into a coffee fund but the company supplied
the kitchen, cooks, tableware, milk, and sugar. Any surplus
which accumulated in the coffee fund was used for various entertainments and summer outings. The dining room contained various

op. cit., p. 79. These restaurant prices compare to the following retail prices which have been taken from a Department
of Commerce and Labor study of retail prices collected as of
February, 1909, from 28 different towns: Coffee, 20¢ to 25¢
per pound; white sugar, 5½¢ to 6¢ per pound; eggs, 27¢ to 32¢
per dozen; butter, 32¢ to 35¢ per pound; milk, 8½¢ to 9½¢ per
quart; beef, 12¢ to 16¢ per pound; pork, 12¢ to 15¢ per pound.
Department of Commerce and Labor, "Cost of Living in the United
States", Bulletin No. 93 (Washington: Government Printing
Office, March, 1911), p. 518.
11 Feiker, F. M., "A Modern Factory Restaurant", Cassier's Magazine, XXX (June, 1906), 160.
12 Frankel, Lee K., and Fleischer, Alexander, op. cit., p. 227.

recreational facilities including a circulating library and an organ. At the close of the meal it was customary to have a five minute talk from some member of the firm, usually a foreman or some executive who discussed departmental problems or the inter-relatedness of the various departments. Visitors were also fre-quently called upon to make remarks.[13]

On the other hand, the eating facilities of the Cleveland Hardware Company were far from elaborate. This company was faced with several complicated problems in its effort to provide a restaurant, but the greatest one was the lack of space. The factory was crowded and every available bit of space was utilized for manufacturing. However, a small room, which had formerly been used as an office, was equipped with a gas stove and desig-nated as the kitchen. In the beginning only coffee and sand-wiches were sold, but when expansion became necessary, the old kitchen was abandoned and converted into a serving room. A new kitchen was built along one wall for a length of 40 or 50 feet. The former dining room was now too small to accommodate the work force. This difficulty was overcome by giving each group of about six men a folding table. Each group appointed one monitor who would take orders from the other members of his group. He would take the basket of his group to the kitchen and place the group's order at eleven o'clock. These baskets were

13 Tolman, William H., Industrial Betterment, p. 10.

then packed by the cooks. The monitor was allowed to stop work
five minutes before the whistle blew to go to the kitchen and take
the basket to where the group had located its table. In this way,
a great rush to the window was avoided when the noon whistle blew.
The company served 400 men in this manner during the day and as
a rule the serving was finished in about ten minutes. Initially,
the office people also ate in the plant. Later a small dining
room was built for them on top of some of the warehouse bins.[14]

William H. Tolman described the kitchen equipment and the
cost of operating this modest attempt to provide hot food to
employees:[15]

> At the start 210-gallon coffee urns were thought
> essential and were provided at a cost of $29 each.
> They are very nice as an ornament, but when a
> man is serving from 50 to 60 gallons of coffee,
> time is too important to wait for it to run out
> of a faucet. 210-gallon cans are now used, which
> cost $3.50 each. A dipper is used in serving the
> coffee. At the start there was a gas stove, but
> a hotel range, the most expensive part of the
> outfit, was put in at a cost of ninety-five dollars.
> Aside from this, the furnishings are simply pots
> and pans of different descriptions, which would
> probably run the expense to another one hundred
> dollars....The head cook is rather a high-priced
> man because he is so experienced that he can take
> the entire management on his own shoulders. He
> is paid $2.50 a day. A girl is paid $3.50 a
> week; these two are on the day turn. They come
> to the factory at about 7 in the morning and
> stay until 4 in the afternoon. The night man
> comes on at 5:30 and stays until 4 in the morning;
> this man is paid $1.50, the price for an ordinary
> cook.

Very frequently recreational facilities were also provided

---

14 Ibid., pp. 20-23.
15 Ibid., p. 21.

with the dining facilities. The Natural Food Company, for example, placed a grand piano at one end of the dining room and
both singing and dancing were permitted during the lunch hour.
The Pope Manufacturing Company of Hartford, Connecticut out-
fitted the lunch room with playing cards, papers, magazines, and
a small library. Warner Brothers, Bridgeport, Connecticut constructed its lunch room in the basement of the Seaside Institute,
which was the employees' club house. This club house was rather
elaborate and provided many recreational facilities for employees.

Administration of Dining Halls

In most instances, firms did not reveal any information
with respect to the administration of lunch rooms and restaurants.
In the absence of any special evidence, it is assumed that
general management absorbed this as part of its duties. However,
several companies did make special provisions for the administration of their dining activities. One of these was the National
Cash Register Company which placed the management of the dining
room, other than the purchase of food, in the hands of the Men's
League. In a formal communication initiating this activity in
1905, the company stated (1) that it would erect the necessary
kitchen, bakery, cold storage rooms, completely equip the dining hall, and furnish recreational facilities, and (2) that no
charge was to be made for rent, breakage, heat, light, services
of the steward, or the services of the purchasing agent. Sidney

Shepard and Company followed a similar plan which was described in the Third Annual Report of the Commissioner of Labor of New York State:[16]

> From the first the entire management of the dining-room has been placed in the hands of the employees; that is, of those who choose to patronize it. Its affairs are conducted by a committee composed of one member from each of the tables in the dining-room (six or eight in 1903), this arrangement giving ample opportunity for discussion and expression of opinion by all those using the dining-room concerning any matters connected with the management. The Committee hires the necessary help (two girls in 1903) to cook, serve the meals, and keep the rooms in order, buy all supplies, make up the menus, etc.

Quite the opposite plan was used by the Plymouth Cordage Company of North Plymouth, Massachusetts which placed the Treasurer in complete charge of the Commissary Department.[17] The John Wanamaker department store of Philadelphia appointed a matron to supervise its dining program. The American Waltham Watch Company placed the supervision of its dining hall in charge of the matron who was also in charge of the boarding house.[18]

The General Electric Company which built and furnished a restaurant at its Schenectady plant contracted with a restauranteur to serve meals at a fixed price.[19] Firms in Rochester, New York engaged a matron to install a restaurant similar to the ones she had successfully introduced into two large high schools in Rochester. She was not only responsible for planning

---

16 Stevens, George A., and Hatch, Leonard W., op. cit., p. 239.
17 Tolman, William H., Social Engineering, p. 84.
18 ibid., p. 79.
19 Feiker, F. M., op. cit., p. 160.

61

all the details with respect to the dining room, but also trained the employees who cooked and served the meals.[20]

Why Dining Facilities Were Provided

Some employers undoubtedly introduced such facilities because they had a genuine concern about the nutritional habits of their employees and viewed hot factory lunches as a possible method of dealing with this problem. This feeling of concern was generally accompanied by a realization that the lack of good food impaired the efficiency of the employees. On this point, Edwin L. Shuey wrote:[21]

> The testimony of all is that the comparatively small amount involved finds abundant return in improved physical condition of workmen and in greater satisfaction. This feature of this topic has been given especial prominence because of the practical character of the methods, the evident return to the employer for his thoughtfulness and the certain improvement of the condition and comfort of the employees.

An employer of some 3,500 employees testified: "I consider that the cost of maintaining our dining hall is more than made up by the increased efficiency of the men and women lunching there."[22] Another employer, W. B. Conkey, President of the W. B. Conkey Company, stated with respect to his restaurant and other activities: "...we believe that we get our returns in dollars and cents."[23]

20 Lattimore, Alida, op. cit., p. 1013.
21 Shuey, Edwin L., op. cit., p. 76.
22 Tolman, William H., Social Engineering, p. 6.
23 Conkey, W. B., "How to Secure Employees' Loyalty," System, VIII, No. 1, (July, 1905), p. 29.

One of the compelling reasons for the introduction of
dining and lunching facilities was that this service could be
offered at little or no cost to employers. Some expense was
obviously entailed in their installation. Many of them, however, were quite inexpensively furnished and the cost was accordingly minimized. Likewise, most firms which supplied meals were
able to recover the major portion of their costs by charging
employees for the food served.[24]

Reasons for the Discontinuance of Eating Facilities

Not all of the dining programs, however, proved to be
successful and the reasons for their discontinuance are of
interest to the student of industrial relations.

Mr. Adams of the Cleveland Hardware Company, in explaining
why his company abandoned its restaurant, said that there were
only 35 employees in his whole company who really wanted one.
More specifically, he commented:[25]

> We think that this could be taken as just about
> the proportion of the seven hundred employes that
> really appreciated the restaurant when it was run
> by the company. This seemed too small a proportion
> to spend fifty or sixty dollars a month on, besides
> a great deal of detail work that is not taken into
> consideration at a money value.

---

24 One employer stated: "When we say our lunch rooms are run
'without loss', we mean that the income from lunches covers
the actual running expenses, in some cases the wear and tear,
repairs, etc. In only one case is the initial cost of the
equipment, or the cost of space, or the interest on the
capital invested reckoned as a cost of running the lunch
room." Quoted in Lattimore, Alida, op. cit., p. 1014.
25 Tolman, William H., Social Engineering, p. 74 and 75.

He added:

> I found in talking with a good many of them about
> the restaurant that they were living in boarding
> houses, and would get no reduction whatever from
> these places on account of not carrying their
> lunches, so no matter what they paid for the
> dinner at the factory, it was entirely an extra
> expense. The keepers of the boarding house would
> tell them that they made preparations for lunches
> anyway, and could not make any reduction on
> account of their not using them.

The Ludlow Manufacturing Company had a similar experience

and J. E. Stevens, Plant Manager, explained the failure of the

program before the Conference on Welfare Work of the National

Civic Federation in these words:[26]

> A substantial but plain dinner is prepared every
> day, consisting of soups, roasts, side dishes,
> ample supply of vegetables, with pie or pudding,
> and tea, coffee, or milk, the whole dinner for
> fifteen cents. This seemed reasonable enough,
> and I think every one is ready to admit that it
> is reasonable. Nevertheless we can hardly feel
> it is a success, because the great masses of the
> people for whom we intended it have never come
> there....One day a man came to me and asked to
> have a house in the village (he was living a
> mile or two away). He said it was too far to go
> home to dinner, and he was tired of eating cold
> lunches. I asked him, just out of curiosity,
> "Why don't you go to the restaurant and get a
> hot dinner for fifteen cents?" He said it was
> too much, as he had to look at every cent. I
> doubt if he had really figured out the gain or
> loss. Still, it certainly remains true that most
> of our men who live at a distance will rather
> stay in the mill and eat a cold lunch than go to
> the restaurant for a hot dinner.

This lack of interest on the part of the employees was

---

26 National Civic Federation, Conference on Welfare Work, op. cit.,
   p. 72.

apparent in several other concerns. Of the 1200 employees of
the Tide Water Oil Works, only fifty men availed themselves
of the room furnished by the company for eating lunch.[27] This
experience was also typical of the Solvay Process Company where
it was estimated that only 250 employees of a possible 2,500
ate at the lunch counter provided by the company.[28]

Generally, however, employees seemed to have been quite
enthusiastic about the dining facilities provided by their
company.

27 Tolman, William H., Industrial Betterment, p. 89.
28 ibid., p. 87.

CHAPTER IV

RECREATION AND EMPLOYEE BENEFITS

Companies had introduced employee recreational activities
prior to 1890. The movement did not get under way, however,
until after 1890.[1] Many of the firms which established such programs were actively engaged in other areas of personnel work.

The recreational efforts embraced a host of activities
conceivable form of indoor recreation to simple reading rooms
or traveling libraries. Not infrequently, large sums of money
were poured into these ventures, particularly where communities
were new or located in isolated areas. In fact, this particular
personnel activity appears to have been given more financial
support than most other personnel programs. The greatest
emphasis was placed on indoor recreation, but baseball fields
were also fitted up, swimming and tennis facilities were sometimes made available, boat trips were arranged, and other outdoor activities were encouraged. A common pattern emerged with
respect to indoor recreation, the nature of which will be set
forth in the following pages.

---

1 William H. Tolman gives the specific dates when seven companies
  originated this social activity. The Illinois Steel Company
  started its program in 1889, but the other six began their
  various clubs between 1901 and 1907. Certainly there were
  other companies, such as the National Cash Register Company,
  which entered this field before 1900. There is no doubt that
  the origin of the vast majority of these programs came into
  being in the years between 1890 and 1910.

Indoor Recreation

Clubs and Social Groups

Employee social organizations were a common feature of
betterment programs and flourished for a multitude of purposes.
In this section, consideration will be limited to organizations
formed to provide recreation and entertainment. Quite frequently
they confined their efforts to one special type of activity.
Many companies had more than one such organization, each operating
independently in a restricted area.

Perhaps the earliest of these employee organizations
originated at the National Cash Register Company which had formed
several social groups for purely recreational purposes as early
as 1899. Among the clubs organized in that year were the Women's
Century Club with 208 members, the Women's Guild having 93
members, the South Park Girls' Literary Club with 140 members,
The Men's Progress Club with 369 members, the Young People's
Club, the Bicycle Club having 90 members, and the Boys' Military
Brigade comprised of 120 members.[2] Such extensive organization
was most unusual and most companies did not support such a wide
variety of social clubs. A much more common practice was for a
company to have one or two specialized clubs. Table I summarizes
the type of activities engaged in by such clubs in nine companies.

---

2 Gilman, Nicholas P., A Dividend to Labor, A Study of Employers'
  Welfare Institutions (Boston: Houghton, Mifflin and Company,
  1899), p. 232.

It will be noted that two of these clubs were exclusively for
management personnel and that the employee groups at times had
both social and educational objectives.

Clubhouses

A number of companies also built clubhouses for their
employees and encouraged varied recreational activities.
Writing in 1900, Edwin L. Shuey said:[3]

> A more permanent method of furnishing pleasure,
> conveniences and instruction is found in the so-
> called "clubhouses" of a number of prominent
> manufacturers. These are usually social and
> educational centers for the employees and their
> families. Some are practically free to the
> working people; others have a fixed fee which
> pays part of the expenses.

Some of these clubhouses were large, beautiful buildings which
furnished facilities for almost every form of recreation.[4]
One of the earliest of these commodious clubhouses, The Seaside
Institute, was erected by the Warner Brothers of Bridgeport,
Connecticut. It has been described as follows:[5]

> On a corner opposite their factory, this
> company erected, in 1887, a clubhouse of the
> first rank for beauty and convenience. This
> is a brick and stone building, presenting a

---

3 Shuey, Edwin L., Factory People and Their Employers (New York:
  Lentilhon & Co., 1900), p. 79.
4 A number of companies prohibited the serving of alcoholic
  beverages. Two companies, the Cleveland Axle Manufacturing
  Company and the Colorado Fuel and Iron Company, stated
  expressly that their purpose in providing a clubhouse was
  to keep the men out of saloons. Other companies permitted
  beer to be served.
5 Shuey, Edwin L., op. cit., p. 80.

Table I

Employee Social Groups

Company	Activities	Approximate Date Formed
John Wanamaker, Philadelphia	"Women's League" - Classes were held in choral singing, physical culture, sewing, dancing, English, French, German, and the mandolin.	n. a.
	"The Looking Forward Club" - Female club for literary and social purposes.	1898
	"The Noonday Club" - For male department heads, buyers and aisle managers.	1899
N. O. Nelson Co.	A Literary Society - Held lectures on literature, history and travel; also had social activities.	1900
Lowe Brothers Co., Dayton, O.	"The High Standard" - A woman's social group.	1901
Plymouth Cordage Company	Girls group, organized to study English, Italian and art.	1901
Westinghouse Electric & Manufacturing Co.	"The Electric Club" - For apprentices and engineers; a social and educational club.	1902
Ludlow Manufacturing Company	"The Ludlow Girls' Institute Association" - Social and athletic club.	1903
Marshall Field & Co.	Choral Society - Public concerts were given.	1907
Natural Food Company	"The Foremen's Club" - Lecture and social group.	n. a.
	"The International Sunshine Club" - A social group for employees.	n. a.
Strawbridge & Clothier	"The Proscenium Club" - Training for expression in speech and action.	n. a.

n. a. Not available

striking architectural effect and is open all
through the day and evening. The original
purpose of this plan was to provide a good
opportunity for a warm lunch for the employees,
as the company has a very large number of women
workers. The building, therefore, contains a
lunch room, with every convenience, on the
lower floor. Above, are parlors, music and
reception rooms, toilet and bath rooms, reading
room and library, a concert hall seating 500
people, amusement rooms and lodging rooms. In
connection with other plans, there are a number
of classes in literature, music, shorthand, and
other subjects of interest and value to women.
In addition, there are sewing machines for the
use of employees doing their own mending and
sewing.

Built at a cost of $60,000, this magnificent building was

formally opened on November 10, 1887 by Mrs. Grover Cleveland.[6]

The clubhouse built by Andrew Carnegie for his employees

in Braddock, Pennsylvania was an outstanding example of the

finest equipment for wholesome recreation. This building which

housed many elaborate devices for employee relaxation and

amusement, was formally opened in January, 1895. The report

of the Department of Commerce and Labor in 1904 contained the

following description:[7]

It has a beautiful theatre, with an ample stage,
full supply of scenery and accessories, and a
seating capacity of 1,200. The swimming pool in
the basement is one of the finest and largest
in the country. The gymansium is spacious, and
is provided with every modern device for the
development of muscle and the promotion of health.
There are also a fine billiard room, containing

---

6 Gilman, Nicholas P., op. cit., p. 262.
7 Hanger, G. W. W., "Housing of the Working People in the United
States", U. S. Department of Commerce and Labor, Bulletin No.
54, (Washington: Government Printing Office, 1904), pp. 1121-2.

> 5 billiard and 4 pool tables, bathrooms, bowling
> alleys, separate bath and billiard rooms for ladies,
> card rooms, reading rooms, instruction rooms for
> classes, and a dark room for developing photo-
> graphs by club members - in fact, the club
> possesses a home perfectly adapted to its needs
> and in every way inviting.
> Courses of lectures and entertainments are
> provided, regardless of expense, which the club
> members have the privilege of attending at
> nominal prices of admission. Educational classes
> are conducted in bookkeeping, shorthand, mechanic-
> al drawing, commercial arithmetic, instrumental
> music, photography, and other subjects, as
> desired, at a cost to club members of 50 cents
> per month.

An equally fine building opened at Homestead in August, 1898,

contained both a library and a clubhouse and was constructed

at a cost of $250,000.[8] The facilities in both cases were

made available to citizens of the community as well as to

employees. The Eagle and Phoenix Club, built before 1900 by

the Eagle and Phoenix Mills of Columbus, Georgia, and the

Steel Works Club, built at a cost of $53,000 by the Illinois

Steel Company in 1889, were among the other truly impressive

clubhouses. The Solvay Process Company had its Guild Hall;

the Westinghouse Electric and Manufacturing Company its

"Casino," and the Peacedale Manufacturing Company its Hazard

Memorial which was built and equipped at a cost of $50,000

in 1891. Other outstanding recreation buildings were provided

by the Gorham Manufacturing Company, the Celluloid Company,

the Cleveland Cliffs-Iron Company, and the Colorado Fuel

---

8 ibid., p. 1122.

and Iron Company.[9]

   With respect to the operation and maintenance of these
recreational buildings, the compamy, in most cases, rendered
the necessary financial assistance. The Eagle and Phoenix
Mills, for example, paid all the general expense and, in
addition, furnished a superintendent, gymnasium director, and
porter for the club.[10] This same procedure was followed by
most companies, although in a few instances, operating
expenses were obtained through small initiation fees and monthly
dues paid by employee members. Typical fees, for example, were
those charged by the Celluloid Company and the Eagle and Phoenix
Mills of a one dollar initial fee and monthly dues of twenty-
five cents.[11] Small charges were also frequently levied for
special courses and lectures.[12]

---

9 More detailed descriptions of all these clubhouses may be
   obtained in Tolman, William H., Social Engineering (New
   York: McGraw-Hill Book Co., 1909); Shuey,Edwin L., op. cit.,
   and National Civic Federation, Proceedings, Conference on
   Welfare Work, (New York: Andrew H. Kellogg Co., 1904).
   These clubhouses were all built between 1889 and 1910.
   Companies which could also be cited for the provision of a
   clubhouse include: the Sherwin-Williams Paint Company, the
   Metropolitan Life Insurance Company, Acme White Lead and
   Color Company, the N. O. Nelson Company, Ludlow Manufacturing
   Company, John B. Stetson Company, the Dodge Manufacturing
   Company, Glendale Elastic Fabrics Company, R. D. Wood Com-
   pany, Iron Clad Manufacturing Company, Proctor Company, New-
   house Mines and Smelter Company, Lynchburg Cotton Mill Com-
   pany, Howland, Croft, Sons and Company, Cheney Brothers, the
   Appollo Iron and Steel Company, the National Elgin Watch Company, the Wilimantic Linen Thread Company, and the S. D.
   Warren Company.
10 Shuey, Edwin L., op. cit. p. 84.
11 ibid., p. 85.
12 Olmstead, Victor H., "The Betterment of Industrial Conditions,"
   U.S. Department of Commerce and Labor, Bulletin No. 31 (Washington: Government Printing Office, 1900), p. 1121.

Only a few companies, among which were the Cleveland Cliffs-
Iron Company and the Westinghouse Electric and Manufacturing
Company, delegated the administration of the building to employee
committees. A unique administrative procedure was adopted by
the Vermont Marble Company which placed the operation of its
$40,000 clubhouse in the hands of the Young Men's Christian
Association. These were decided variations from the usual practice, which was for management to assume the administration and
much of the cost of operating the clubhouse.[13]

Clubhouse facilities were established within the plant by
the Roycroft Shop, the H. J. Heinz Company, and the T. B. Laycock Company.[14] The Heinz Company converted the third and fourth
floors of the factory into an auditorium capable of seating
2,500 people.[15] This auditorium was made available to the
community and was placed at the disposal of the employees for
entertainments, lectures, social occasions and concerts. It
also served as a noon meeting place where the employees
collected for talks by visitors and department heads.[16]

One outstanding feature of many of these recreation

13 National Civic Federation, Conference on Welfare Work, op.
   cit., p. 182.
14 Shuey, Edwin L., op. cit., p. 76.
15 Tolman, William H., Social Engineering, p. 11. The Heinz
   Company also provided a roof garden situated on top of the
   building.
16 Shuey, Edwin L., op. cit., p. 76.

buildings was the inclusion of a fully-equipped gymnasium.[17]
A typical gymnasium in use at the Illinois Steel Company, for
example, was 45 feet square and was adjoined by a handball
court, bowling alley, 16 bathrooms and 6 shower baths.[18] The
company also employed a director of physical activity to supervise athletic activities.

Discussing the gymnasium in his company, J. E. Stevens,
Plant Manager of the Ludlow Manufacturing Company, stated:[19]

> Of the things we have undertaken, that which
> has succeeded best is the men's gymnasium.
> This is entirely self-supporting. We started
> this men's club in a small way, simply furnish-
> ing the room, the light, and the heat. We got
> the men to manage it themselves from the start.
> They established their own committees, and
> have managed their own affairs ever since. It
> has been a success financially also, and beyond
> what I have stated, we have not been called on
> to contribute anything for several years.

As a general rule, the formation of an athletic association
was a concomitant development and frequently encompassed a
separate organization for women.[20] Modest contributions by
members were usual and helped defray operational costs.

Libraries and Reading Rooms

In 1856, the Peacedale Manufacturing Company constructed a
building to accommodate a library which had been established

---

17 One of the first companies to construct a gymnasium for the
   use of its employees was the P. Lorillard Company in 1882.
   (Gilman, Nicholas P., op. cit.. p. 291).
18 Olmstead, Victor H., op. cit., p. 1119.
19 From an address given before the Conference on Welfare Work
   of the National Civic Federation in 1904.
20 Olmstead, Victor H., op. cit., p. 1121.

two years earlier, and in 1878 the Ludlow Manufacturing Company instituted a library for its employees.[21] By 1909, a library had become a common practice. The library or reading room was an almost universal feature of employee clubhouses. Moreover, companies which did not provide such elaborate facilities, often made special reading rooms or library facilities available. The objective seems to have been to provide employees with a place in which to obtain enjoyment and improve their general knowledge. Some employers also regarded the library as a means whereby workers could prepare themselves for promotion.[22] Frequently, these facilities served as the headquarters for the educational and literary organizations of the company. The importance attached by the S. D. Warren & Company to its library is set forth below:[23]

> A free library and reading room, maintained by
> the company, is an important educational factor
> in the community. This contains about 4,000
> volumes of standard reading matter, in addition
> to which are found all the leading magazines
> and other publications. It is situated on
> the second floor of the building in which the
> company's offices are located, and is much
> frequented by the employees. The original cost
> of the library was about $5,000 and some $300
> a year is required to defray running expenses.
> A literary society, composed of women employees,
> meets regularly in the library.

The library of the Peacedale Manufacturing Company, the Colorado Fuel and Iron Company, and that of the Cleveland Cliffs-Iron Company served the community as well as the employees.

---

21 Hanger, G. W. W., op. cit., p. 1221.
22 Tolman, William H., Social Engineering, p. 8.
23 Hanger, G. W. W., op. cit., p. 1241.

Cheney Brothers, a silk firm, donated a free public library to the town of South Manchester, Connecticut.[24] The library of the Plymouth Cordage Company was not only placed at the disposal of the whole community but the librarian, as is evident from the following description, served the community in other ways:[25]

> Situated on a hill overlooking the houses and the mill is the Loring Reading Room, which was presented to the company by Mr. Augustus P. Loring, now president of the company, as a memorial to his father, Caleb William Loring, who held the office before him, and who, at the time of his last visit to Plymouth, had expressed his desire to do something which would add to the happiness and welfare of the operatives in the mills....The library contains 4,000 volumes of fiction, history and travel, and is in charge of a trained librarian and assistant. The librarian spends part of the time visiting the people and the schools to help and cooperate with them in their work. Books are sent to the sick; also, books which are not contained in the library may be procured from any other library.

Some employers contributed generously to public libraries and in return were frequently permitted the privilege of opening a branch public library within the confines of the plant. As a rule, a room was set aside to accommodate this function, but such was not always the case. At the National Cash Register Company, the library was brought to the men. At noon, books and magazines were conveyed through the factory so that employees could select suitable reading matter. This service was rendered by a nearby branch station of the city public library.[26]

---

24 Gilman, Nicholas P., op. cit., p. 258.
25 Hanger, G. W. W., op. cit., p. 1228.
26 Tolman, William H., Industrial Betterment (New York: The Social Service Press, 1900), p. 28.

The Cleveland Hardware Company had a similar arrangement with the Cleveland Public Library but the method of distribution was somewhat different. Lists of available books were posted. The worker gave the title of the book he wanted to the time-keeper who saw to it that it was ordered from the library.[27]

An additional feature, often introduced along with libraries, was a special room set aside for lounging, resting, and reading. This feature was quite popular even in the absence of a library. It usually contained newspapers and periodicals. The A. B. Chase Company provided a reading room which, in addition to magazines and newspapers, was supplied with writing desks, paper, pens, and ink.[28] Joseph Bancroft and Sons Company, among others, introduced a reading room primarily for use during the lunch hour. The Brooklyn Eagle Newspaper provided a room where drivers and employees of the circulation department could relax between runs.[29] The Denver City Tramway Company, the Chicago City Railway, and the Brooklyn Rapid Transit company had

---

27 ibid., p. 32. In addition to the companies previously men-
    tioned, separate libraries were provided by: The Waltham
    Watch Company, the First National Bank of Chicago, The
    Brooklyn Daily Eagle, the Weston Electrical Instrument
    Company, the Wanamaker Department Store, Philadelphia, Pope
    Manufacturing Company, the Potter Printing Press, McAden
    Mills, the P. Lorillard and Company, and the Wells-Fargo
    Company. The last mentioned company placed the entire
    management of the library in the hands of the employees.
28 ibid., p. 17.
29 Tolman, William H., Social Engineering, p. 309.

similar off-duty arrangements for their employees.[30] Frequently these rooms served as rest rooms during the day, particularly for female workers, and as emergency rooms for injured or sick workers. Sometimes dancing was permitted after lunch, music being supplied by a piano or victrola.[31] The Natural Food Company, the Gorham Manufacturing Company, and the Ferris Brothers Company also maintained such facilities.

Contribution of the Young Men's Christian Association

The Y. M. C. A. frequently provided recreational programs for employees, particularly railroad workers. In 1872, it established its first railroad branch, designed to provide wholesome recreation and entertainment. By 1900, there were 118 Y. M. C. A. railroad branches throughout the country. All of these branches supplied current periodical literature; 105 branches provided bathrooms; 97 visited sick and injured members; 56 maintained rest rooms and sleeping accommodations; 36 provided gymnasiums, and 95 had libraries containing a total of 70,000 volumes.[32] Land, buildings, and about 60 per cent of the cost of operating these branches were generally provided by the company.[33] One railroad official was quoted as stating that - "If you vote this money for this purpose (Y. M. C. A.

---

30 Gilman, Nicholas P., op. cit., p. 281.
31 Frankel, Lee K., and Fleischer, Alexander, The Human Factor
   in Industry (New York: The MacMillan Company, 1920), p. 240.
32 Olmstead, Victor H., op. cit., p. 1155-6.
33 ibid.

branches) it means more to the company than the same amount would if invested in steel rails."[34]

Other Indoor Activities

Musical organizations were introduced by a limited number of companies. The Natural Food Company described its company band as follows:[35]

> The band is a musical organization consisting of thirty pieces. All employees of the company who can play any band instrument are eligible to membership, and at the same time a number of players in the city are included in the organization. The band is under the charge of a competent leader, who was formerly in charge of the regimental band of this city. Rehearsals are held once a week, and a number of engagements are secured. It is really a very creditable organization. Uniforms are provided, and the company donates a certain sum each year for the maintenance of this organization.

The N. O. Nelson Company also organized and financed a band of 30 members which performed two nights a week during the summer on the spacious lawn of the plant.[36] Among the other companies which encouraged musical organizations were the Pope Manufacturing Company, the Plymouth Cordage Company, and the Gorham Manufacturing Company.

Outdoor Recreation

Sports

Outdoor recreational facilities for employees did not

---

34 ibid.
35 National Civic Federation, Conference on Welfare Work, op. cit., p. 161.
36 Olmstead, Victor H., op. cit., p. 1141.

command the interest or enthusiasm that was lavished on indoor
programs. However, athletic fields for outdoor sports were
built by a few companies, and others cooperated with the Young
Men's Christian Association or arranged with private athletic
clubs for the use of their outdoor facilities.[37] The Solvay
Process Company enclosed a five-acre plot beside its office
building for the purpose of encouraging physical culture through
outdoor sports. This model athletic field was used for tennis,
baseball, and track events.[38] The Natural Food Company also
constructed a private park for outdoor sports. The Plymouth
Cordage Company, in addition to an athletic field, maintained
a bathing beach for employees along the shore of Plymouth Bay.[39]
Other companies that made provision for outdoor recreational
activities included the Ludlow Manufacturing Company, the Pelzer
Manufacturing Company, the United States Shoe Company, Briarcliff
Farms, L. O. Koven and Brothers Company, the Proctor Company,
and the International Harvester Company. The Weston Electrical
Instrument Company constructed a large swimming pool under its
employee dining hall in 1903.[40]

Outings and Picnics

As early as 1870, the Conant Thread Company furnished

37 Shuey, Edwin L., op. cit., p. 56.
38 National Civic Federation, Conference on Welfare Work,
   op. cit., p. 187.
39 Hanger, G. W. W., op. cit., p. 1232.
40 Tolman, William H., Social Engineering, p. 66.

transportation for its employees to a beach resort and, although
the employees were not paid for the day, they were treated to
a free dinner by the company.[41] This type of benefit continued
to enjoy favor with a number of other companies into the period
under consideration. In 1899, Oneida Community, Ltd. instituted
their annual custom of financing an outing to a summer resort
and several other firms were reported by the New York State
Department of Labor in 1903 to have followed a similar practice.[42]
Employees were not remunerated for this holiday. The Proximity
Manufacturing Company instituted the practice of an annual outing
in 1906. A list of companies which held such outings would in-
clude the Kinnard Manufacturing Company, Strawbridge and Clothier
Department Store, the Gus Blass Dry Goods Company of Little
Rock, the Metropolitan Street Railway Company, the Cincinatti
Milling Machine Company, and the Brooklyn Rapid Transit Company.[43]
A most novel innovation was provided by the National Cash Register
Company which closed its factory for two weeks in 1904 and paid
part of the expenses of 2200 employees to the St. Louis Expo-
sition.[44] In 1905 and 1906 the Men's Welfare League of this
same company arranged for an eight-day outing at Port Huron,
Michigan.[45] The expenses of this trip, $7.80, were presumably

41 Tolman, William H., Industrial Betterment, p. 318.
42 Stevens, George A., and Hatch, Leonard W., "Employers' Welfare
   Institutions," Third Annual Report of the Commissioner of
   Labor, New York State Department of Labor, (1904), p. 299.
43 Gilman, Nicholas P., op. cit., p. 282.
44 Tolman, William H., Social Engineering, p. 277.
45 ibid., p. 318.

paid by the employees.

Miscellaneous Services

Vacations

Vacations with pay were sometimes granted by some employers in this period. These opportunities for rest, as they were frequently designated, were usually one or two weeks' duration. Quite frequently they were related to length of service, although at the Atlantic Division of the Wells-Fargo Company, the vacation period ranged from three days to a month, depending upon the position of the employee.[46] The Volkman, Stollwerck and Company of New York was an early leader in providing annual vacations. In 1890, this company granted one week's vacation with pay to employees with at least one year's service. Distinct variations in vacation policies appeared. At the Shepard Company, for instance, each employee with at least one year's service was granted a two weeks' vacation with pay and the social secretary was authorized to help employees in financing their vacation in cases where she felt such aid was warranted.[47] Another unusual policy with respect to vacations was followed by the Curtis Publishing Company which used this benefit as a device to reduce lateness and absenteeism. The following

46 An outline of this company's program was presented by E. A. Stedman, Manager of the company, at the Conference on Welfare Work of the National Civic Federation.
47 National Civic Federation, Conference on Welfare Work, op. cit., p. 112.

description of this program appeared in 1909:[48]

> As a stimulus to daily promptness and regularity
> in attendance, the Curtis Publishing Company in
> making up the vacation list gives preference to
> those clerks who have the best record for
> attendance and punctuality. Each absence counts
> two points, and each lateness of less than one
> hour, one point, against the record of any
> clerk. The employees having the least number
> of points against them have first choice in the
> selection of vacation time....Employees who
> have been connected with the company for at
> least six months are entitled to a vacation
> at a convenient time, between June first and
> September first in each year; but no vacation
> in any case exceeds two weeks, unless at the
> expense of such employee and with the approval
> of the proper bureau manager or officer.

The technique of using paid vacations to stimulate more regular
attendance also found favor with the C. Howard Hunt Pen Company
and the James R. Keiser Company. The former company allowed
one day's vacation for each month worked without absence.[49]
Paid vacations were also a part of the personnel program of
the National Cash Register Company, the Acme Sucker Rod Company,
the Ferris Brothers Company, the New York Telephone Company,
the Brooklyn Bridge Railway, the New York Edison Company,
Strawbridge and Clothier Department Store, Blanchard and Price,
and the Siegel-Cooper Department Store. The program of the last
mentioned company was eloquently described by William H. Tolman:[50]

> The steamer Republic every Saturday morning
> carried eighty girls from the store to Long
> Branch. The party was in charge of a matron,

48 Tolman, William H., Social Engineering, p. 7.
49 ibid., p. 8.
50 Tolman, William H., Industrial Betterment, p. 38.

who saw her protegees safely landed in the Wheeler
Cottage, where a week of solid, health-restoring
enjoyment, free from all financial worry or
business cares, was enjoyed.....Every indoor amusement ever devised was at hand should inclement
weather forbid outing trips. Lawn tennis and
croquet grounds attracted the athletic girls,
while dreamy hammocks and big, embracing, sleep-
inducing chairs under the shade of tall trees in-
vited tranquil rest. How the hard-working girls
enjoyed this week of rest and freedom can be
only imagined, while the strength gained and
stored up against the fatiguing demands of the
other busy fifty-one can hardly be overestimated.

Other Miscellaneous Services

Some firms followed the policy of distributing gifts to
employees on special occasions. At its annual Christmas party,
for instance, the John B. Stetson Company gave each man either
a turkey or a hat and each woman a pair of gloves and a box of
candy.[51] The Cincinnati Milling Machine Company also distributed
turkeys at Christmas and the Knoth Brothers in New York City
presented gifts of money.[52]

One of the more common services provided by employers
was the installation of racks and sheds to house the bicycles
used by the workers to get to work.[53] In 1899, the J. H.
Williams and Company provided bleachers so that employees of

---

51 At the Christmas party in 1908, the company gave away 358
hats, 1711 turkeys, 902 pairs of gloves, 100 pounds of
candy, 62 watches, and 60 chains. (Reported in Tolman,
William H., Social Engineering, p. 302.)
52 Stevens, George A., and Hatch, Leonard W., op. cit., p. 286.
53 ibid., p. 251.

the firm might view the Dewey parade.[54] Another unusual service
was the steam-heated greenhouse maintained by the N. O. Nelson
Company where residents could secure plants and flowers free
of charge and also avail themselves of the services of the landscape gardener.[55] Quite unique too, was the park carriage furnished by the H. J. Heinz Company for use by the company's
women employees during the summer.[56]

Conclusion

There was a widespread interest during this twenty-year
period in employee recreation programs and employee benefits,
and many employers backed up that interest with substantial
financial outlays. In part, these programs were the outgrowth
of a sincere interest in employee comfort and health. In part,
they were inspired by the desire to build employee morale and
to achieve greater productivity. The absence of community
recreation facilities may have also been a factor. Of interest
is the explanation given by William H. Tolman of the reasons
which led to their introduction:[57]

> The general attitude of employers is quite
> different from that of one who remarked that
> in his business they used up a man every six
> years and then hired new ones. Men are saved
> and not used up. They are beginning to wonder
> what their employees do with their spare time
> outside of their working hours in the factory,
> how they spend their evenings, what kind of

54 Shuey, Edwin L., op. cit., p. 128.
55 Olmstead, Victor H., op. cit., p. 1140.
56 Tolman, William H., Industrial Betterment, p. 11.
57 ibid., p. 37.

recreation they have and so on. They again
realize their identity of interest, for it is
far better that the employee uses his outside
time so as to make him more ready for work
on the morrow, rather than that he should do
all sorts of things that will dissipate his
strength, energy and moral fibre. Accordingly,
movements for recreation are of importance.

CHAPTER V

HOURS, INCENTIVE WAGE PLANS, AND SUPPLEMENTARY
COMPENSATION

This chapter will deal with hours of work, incentive
wage plans, and measures to provide supplementary compensation.
Emphasis will be placed on the techniques which were used to
induce employees to put forth greater effort on the job.
Important among the changes introduced by employers were incentive wage plans. Straight piece rate systems had been used
long before 1890, but more refined plans were an integral
feature of the Scientific Management Movement which had its
beginning in this period.

It was also in this period that profit sharing and employee
stock ownership plans were tested out as devices to reduce
friction and misunderstanding. Suggestion systems, designed to
bring forth ideas of value to the company, also became increas-
ingly popular. Some firms chose to share the growing income of
their business by establishing pension plans and through
cooperative purchasing for employees, while others elected to
provide more leisure by shortening the hours of work. The
trend toward shorter hours will be reviewed. Thereafter,
consideration will be given to incentive wage plans and supplementary compensation programs.

Hours of Labor

The American Federation of Labor, like the Knights of

86

Labor, was vitally interested in reducing the hours of work.
Since its formation in 1881, it had made the eight-hour day
its rallying cry. Little progress was made during the eighties.
In 1890, the average employee in manufacturing industries worked
60 hours a week. Table I shows that the unions made little
headway during the nineties. In 1900, the granite workers won
its strike for an eight-hour day. Thereafter, weekly hours
began a gradual decline. In 1904, the International Typographical Union inaugurated its nation-wide movement for the
eight-hour day.[1] Other unions met with some success in reducing
their hours of work.

Chester W. Wright estimated that in 1890 the average
working day was slightly over 11 hours.[2] In 1910, instead of
a standard work week of 60 hours which had prevailed at the
beginning of the period, the standard stood at 56.6 hours.[3]
On the basis of a six-day week, this meant a decline from 10
to slightly more than 9 hours per working day. Bryce M. Stewart
estimated that only about 12 per cent of the wage earners in all
manufacturing industries worked forty-eight or less hours per
week in 1914.[4] The movement toward shorter weekly hours lagged

---

1 Peterson, Florence, Survey of Labor Economics (New York: Harper
  & Brothers, 1947), p. 436.
2 Wright, Chester W., Economic History of the United States (New
  York: McGraw-Hill Book Company, 1941), p. 720. As will be
  noted in subsequent figures, estimates of the average work
  day varied slightly.
3 Peterson, Florence, op. cit., p. 436.
4 Stewart, Bryce M., Development of Industrial Relations in the
  United States (New York: Industrial Relations Counselors, Inc.,
  1949), p. 19.

in the steel industry. The United States Steel Company, for
example, increased its weekly hours from 68.4 hours in 1902
to 68.9 in 1913.[5]

Table I

Average Hours per Week in All Manufacturing Industries[1]

Year	Average Hours	Year	Average Hours
1890	60.0	1900	59.0
1891	59.7	1901	58.7
1892	59.8	1902	58.3
1893	59.7	1903	57.9
1894	59.1	1904	57.7
1895	59.5	1905	57.7
1896	59.2	1906	57.3
1897	59.1	1907	57.3
1898	59.3	1908	56.8
1899	59.1	1909	56.8

1 Adapted from Douglas, Paul H., Real Wages in the United States,
  1890 - 1926 (Boston: Houghton Mifflin Company, 1930), p. 116.

It should be noted, as Paul H. Douglas has pointed out,
that there was considerable variation in working time from
industry to industry, and a significant difference between
unionized industries and those which were virtually unorganized.
Average weekly hours in union industries moved from 54.4 hours
in 1890 to 50.1 hours in 1910. During this same period, however,

---

5 ibid. A government survey which was completed in May, 1910 and
  covered 172,671 employees in the steel industry disclosed that
  nearly one-half of these workers were employed seventy-two
  hours a week or more--at least twelve hours daily on the basis
  of six days per week. Nearly all the workers were employed
  eighty-four hours or more per week. (Reported in Goldmark,
  Josephine, Fatigue and Efficiency [New York: Survey Associates,
  Inc., 1912], p. 4)

weekly hours outside the unionized industries decreased from
62.2 hours in 1890 to only 59.8 hours in 1910.[6]

Experience of Several Companies

Some companies were much more progressive than others in
their approach to hours of work in this period in which legislation bearing on working time was almost non-existent.[7] Fels
and Company, soap manufacturers of Philadelphia, which employed
about 175 people, was a pioneer in this field. Nicholas P.
Gilman reported in 1899 that several years earlier, the working
day for men in this company had been reduced from ten to nine
hours. Later, the day for girls and women was reduced to eight
hours, and the day for men and boys was also curtailed in dull
periods without any reduction in pay. The work week for men
was five and one-half days and five days for women.[8] About this
time, the Lever Brothers' Company instituted a similar policy
and, in 1897, the Acme Sucker Rod Company instituted a fifty-
hour week.[9] About 1900, the National Cash Register Company

---

6 Douglas, Paul H., op. cit., pp. 112-115. Union industries
included the metal trades, granite and stone, book and job
printing, newspaper printing, planing mills and bakers. The
"payroll" industries, where hours were much longer, included
cotton, boots and shoes, clothing, hosiery and knit goods,
woolens, lumber (sawmills), iron and steel and slaughtering
and meatpacking.
7 Massachusetts had passed a ten hour statute as early as 1879,
but little legislative activity occurred in this area until the
constitutionality of such legislation had been affirmed by the
Supreme Court in 1908. Legislation had also been enacted
regulating the hours of certain government employees.
8 Gilman, Nicholas P., A Dividend to Labor, A Study of Employers'
Welfare Institutions (Boston: Houghton, Mifflin and Company,
1899), p. 288.
9 Olmstead, Victor H., "The Betterment of Industrial Conditions",

reduced the hours of its female labor from ten to eight.[10]
In March, 1901, the J. H. Williams Company voluntarily reduced
the working time of its employees from ten hours to nine without
a corresponding decrease in wage rates, and the Cassidy & Son
Manufacturing Company did likewise a year later.[11] Included
also among the firms which had a liberal policy on hours of
work were the Enterprise Manufacturing Company, the Natural
Food Company, the Peacedale Manufacturing Company, the United
States Playing Card Company, and the Westinghouse Electric and
Manufacturing Company.

The motivation for shorter hours of work was not pure
philanthropy. Several studies had been made which corroborated
the assertion that shorter hours did not always result in
smaller output but actually increased it. As early as 1873, the
factual testimony of the treasurer of the Atlantic Mills at
Lawrence, Massachusetts before the Massachusetts Committee on
Labor substantiated this claim.[12] Josephine Goldmark summarized
the results of one study: "Six years after the Massachusetts
ten-hour law went into effect, a full investigation under Carroll
D. Wright showed that the cost of production had not been in-

U.S. Department of Commerce and Labor, Bulletin No. 31 (Washington: Government Printing Office, 1900), p. 1137.
10 Shuey, Edwin L., Factory People and Their Employers (New York:
Lentilhon & Co., 1900), p. 113.
11 Stevens, George A., and Hatch, Leonard W., "Employers' Welfare
Institutions," Third Annual Report of the Commissioner of
Labor, New York State Department of Labor, (1904), p. 265.
12 Goldmark, Josephine, op. cit., p. 170.

creased, nor had wages been lowered under the Massachusetts ten-
hour day....The worker's increased efficiency more than balanced
the curtailment of working time."[13] Studies of this nature undoubtedly provided a partial explanation for the reduction in
hours of work. Considerable hostility toward shorter hours prevailed during this period. As late as 1902, the president of the
National Association of Manufacturers denounced an eight-hour
bill as being socialistic and circumscribing the inalienable
right of an individual to use his time as he saw fit.[14] Despite
this sort of opposition and the argument that leisure time tended
to destroy health and morals, the chief basis of employer opposition centered on the fear that such moves would increase
the costs of production.[15] Regardless of the reason, the movement toward shorter hours was slow to gain momentum.

Incentive Wage Payment Plans

The growth of incentive wage payment plans, other than piece-
rates, was closely tied to the development of Scientific Management in this early period. In fact, the setting of wages in a
more scientific manner was an expressed goal of the pioneers of
this movement. In a paper entitled "Shop Management" presented
at a meeting of the American Society of Mechanical Engineers
in 1903, Frederick W. Taylor argued that the first object of

---

13 ibid., p. 131.
14 Parry, D. M., Disastrous Effects of a National Eight-Hour
   Law, Pamphlet, 1902.
15 Peterson, Florence, op. cit., p. 425.

management is to unite high wages with low labor costs.

Straight Piece Rate Systems

The use of piece rates had accompanied the introduction of the factory system. In 1889, Nicholas P. Gilman wrote: "Piece work is practiced in many industries. Where it is not applicable throughout the manufacture, it is extended to all the processes in which it is feasible."[16] The extensive use of piece rates is understandable because employers quickly perceived that benefits would accrue to both themselves and workers under such a system. It gave an incentive to ambitious, energetic workmen who, by producing more, could increase their daily earnings and, at the same time, lower the unit costs of production. A study conducted by Professor McCabe in 1908 gives some indication of the extent to which piece wages were used. His study of 117 unions involving 1,687,300 members showed that about twenty-eight per cent of the employees were working under some type of piece-rate system.[17]

Incentive Wage Systems

F. W. Taylor first used a stop-watch to measure performance in a steel plant in 1881. It was this and similar studies that gave rise to experimentation with wage incentives. Within a

---

16 Gilman, Nicholas P., Profit Sharing between Employer and Employee (Boston: Houghton, Mifflin and Company, 1889), p. 47.
17 Cited in Slichter, Sumner H., Union Policies and Industrial Management (Washington: The Brookings Institution, 1941), p. 286.

short time, Taylor devised the first formal incentive wage system.[18]
This "Differential Rate System", as it was called, modified the
straight piece-rate plan by setting two distinct sets of piece
rates for each job -- a lower piece rate when less than the
established day's task was completed and a higher rate per piece
when total output equaled or exceeded the established task.
About 1890, Frederick A. Halsey, an outstanding industrial
engineer for the Yale and Towne Manufacturing Company, devised
the Halsey Gain-Sharing Plan. This was the first incentive
system to provide a guaranteed rate plus a premium for extra
output, and its origin has been traced to the profit sharing
plan introduced by Henry R.Towne in 1886.[19] It was not until
about 1898, however, that the plan engendered any real interest.
The Gantt Task and Bonus Plan, which combined the characteristics
of both the Taylor and the Halsey plans, was introduced by Henry
L. Gantt, an associate of F. W. Taylor, at the Bethlehem Steel
Works in 1901.[20] This plan, like the Halsey plan, provided a
guaranteed minimum wage for output below the "task", instead
of the Taylor punitive low piece rate. Above the "task", the
worker received not merely the equivalent of full piece rates
instead of a portion as under the Halsey plan, but also an
additional premium which was similar to the high piece rate
under the Taylor plan. Another important incentive wage-

---

18 Stewart, Bryce M., op. cit., p. 19.
19 Peterson, Florence, op. cit., p. 340. A somewhat similar
   plan was devised in 1898 by James Rowan of the David Rowan
   and Company,Glasgow, Scotland.
20 ibid., p. 341.

payment plan, the Emerson Efficiency Bonus System, was first put
into operation by Harrington Emerson on the Santa Fe Railroad
in 1904.[21] The unique feature of the Emerson Efficiency Bonus
System was its provision for premium rates to begin at approximately 70 per cent of standard, with graduated rates thereafter
reaching to 120 per cent at standard, after which the rate remained constant. These systems were, in part designed to offset
the rather strenuous objections which had been made by the Knights
of Labor over the common practice of cutting piece rates.[22]

One of the firms that had adopted the Halsey plan was the
Cincinnati Milling Machine Company. In 1909, after seven years'
experience with this plan, a member of management was quoted as
saying:[23]

> The basis of a successful premium plan, is of course
> a fair setting of the time....It should be understood
> with the workman in advance that if a manufacturer
> contributes anything directly toward reduction in the
> time by supplying an improved machine, or improved
> jigs or fixtures--that then it would be perfectly
> proper and fair to lower the time set.
> On the other hand, this time should not be lowered
> by the manufacturer just because a workman, through
> his own individual skill, has arrived at a point where
> his earnings grow considerably beyond the ordinary
> rate.

Because this underlying philosophy did not prevail generally,
strong worker resistance was encountered.

---

21 ibid., p. 342.
22 Lytle, Charles, W., Wage Incentive Methods (New York: The
   Ronald Press, 1942), p. 201.
23 Quoted in Tolman, William H., Social Engineering (New York:
   McGraw-Hill Book Company, 1909), p. 228.

A number of firms including the Providence Engineering
Works and the Chambersburg Engineering Company, adopted premium
plans successfully but the Miller, DuBrul and Peters Manufacturing
Company, which had installed the Halsey Plan in 1903, abandoned
it several years later because the work had changed and had become irregular.[24] Many firms were reluctant to replace their
straight piece-rate system with incentive wage plans. As late
as 1924, a survey of 175 manufacturing establishments employing
220,536 wage earners disclosed that only 28,173 or 12.7 per cent
were being paid by means of bonus or premium plans.[25]

Miscellaneous Financial Incentives

The incentive system used by the Sherwin-Williams Paint
Company was described in 1904 by Mr. Albright of that company
before the Conference on Welfare Work:[26]

> We have what we call the "top notch" system,
> something I haven't heard of here today. That
> system exists in all the different departments
> of our institution. It is made up by points,
> governing the different departments. For
> instance, we have eight or nine managers for
> our different houses. At the end of the year
> the manager who has made the most points or
> profit, from the office of manager, is called
> the "top notch" manager, and with that top
> notch he has a check of $500 added to his
> salary. That system is followed right down

24 ibid., p. 231.
25 Slichter, Sumner H., "Competitive Exchange as a Method of
   Interesting Workmen in Output and Costs", American Economic
   Review, XV, No. 1, Supplement, (March, 1925), p. 94. Another
   study made by the National Industrial Conference Board in
   1924 showed that only 7.3% of the workers studied were under
   premium or bonus plans.
26 National Civic Federation, Proceedings, Conference on Welfare
   Work (New York: Andrew H. Kellogg Co., 1904), p. 133.

to the boy who sweeps out the rooms; it goes
through every department. They have also
presented to them a little gold badge with a
"T. N." on it, which they are supposed to
wear for the year.

A few companies, including the John B. Stetson Company and the

Gorham Manufacturing Company, made special awards to apprentices

upon successful completion of their course of study. The former

company gave a sum equal to $1 for every week spent in training,

or $208 for the full four-year period.[27] The rewards made to

apprentices at the Gorham Manufacturing Company were based on

their performance in the course.[28]

The Stetson Company also experimented with the use of

incentives to discourage labor turnover. This system was quite

unique as can be seen from the following description:[29]

A novel feature introduced by the company in
1897 was the adoption of a system of premiums
for regular and faithful work in the sizing
department, where the roving habits of the
workmen, many of whom were of foreign birth,
had become a source of serious annoyance and
inconvenience to the management. To remedy
these conditions it was decided to offer to
the men who worked steadily throughout the
year an amount equal to 5 per cent of the total
wages earned, this amount to be presented to
such employees in the form of a Christmas gift.
Under the operation of this plan 35 per cent
of the sizers employed in 1897 remained until
the end of the year. For the three succeeding

27 Hanger, G. W. W., "Housing of the Working People in the United
   States", United States Department of Commerce and Labor,
   Bulletin 54, September, 1904, p. 1238.
28 National Civic Federation, Conference on Welfare Work, op. cit.,
   p. 101.
29 Hanger, G. W. W., op. cit., p. 1237.

years the premium was increased to 10 per cent,
with the result that the number of steady workers
increased from 50 to 80 per cent of the entire
number. In 1901 and 1902, with 15 per cent premium paid, the percentage reached 88, while
last year 92 per cent of the total force in the
sizing department received 20 per cent increase
on their wages as a reward for faithful service.

Profit Sharing

Sharing profits with employees was early recognized as

one possible way of reducing conflict between employers and

employees over wages and working conditions. It was also

optimistically viewed as a means of stimulating the employee

to increase production, improve quality, and reduce waste so

that total profits and, therefore, his share of those profits

would be increased. Profit sharing antedates the period under

consideration by many years. The first isolated attempt

probably was that made by Albert Gallatin at his New Geneva,

Pennsylvania glass works in 1794.[30] The experiment was evidently

of short duration. Any attempt to trace the history of this

method of remuneration is made more difficult by the tendency

to include a variety of supplementary wage plans under this

heading.

Early Attempts at Profit Sharing

The publicity given to the profit sharing plan of the

Whitwood Collieries, England, which was in effect from 1865

---

30 Gilman, Nicholas P., Profit Sharing Between Employer and Employee, p. 296.

to 1875, undoubtedly influenced American thinking on the subject.
One of the pioneer attempts in this country was made by Brewster
and Company, carriage builders of New York. In their statement
announcing the plan to their employees on October 9, 1869,
the company stated: "From the beginning of our fiscal year, we
offer to all persons in our employ, excepting those now having
an interest in our business, a certain share of our annual
profits, in addition to the regular wages, which we propose
shall be no less than the highest wages paid in similar
establishments."[31] In the spring of 1871, however, the
employees engaged in a strike for an eight-hour working day.
Management felt that the spirit of the plan had been violated
and in June of that year dissolved the "partnership," thus
ending the experiment.[32] A much more successful experiment was
begun in 1869 by the A. S. Cameron and Company of Jersey City
which was continued until Mr. Cameron's death in 1877.[33] Most
of the plans in these earlier years were short-lived. In
1889, Nicholas P. Gilman summarized the reasons for the failures
of plans which had been instituted to that date. Eleven
companies were reported to have attempted plans in this general
area without success. Their experience is recorded in Table II.

---

31 Quoted in Tolman, William H., Social Engineering, p. 201.
32 Adams, Thomas S., and Sumner, Helen L., Labor Problems
   (New York: The Macmillan Company, 1905), p. 358.
33 ibid.

Table II[1]

Name of Establish-ment, Place and Nature of Business	Date	Number of Employees	Cause of Change
Bay State Shoe & Leather Co., Worchester	1867-73	- -	Strike in 1 room; no improvement
A. S. Cameron & Co., Steam Pump Mfrs., New York	1869-77	- -	Death of Mr. Cameron in 1877
Brewster & Co., Carriage Mfrs., New York	1870-72	450	8-hour strike in 1872
Lister Bros., Fertilizer Works, Newark, N. J.	1882	- -	Results not satisfactory
Norton Bros., Mfrs. Sheetmetal goods, Chicago, Ill.	1886	- -	"Force not intelligent enough"
N. E.Granite Works, Westerly, R. I.	1886	350 to 500	Advance in wages
L. H. Williams, Builder, New York, N. Y.	1886	- -	Mr. Williams died in 1887
Union (Coal) Mining Co., Mt. Savage, Md.	1886-87	300	No improvement; Strike
Welshans & McEwan, Plumbers, Omaha, Neb.	1886-87	30	Trouble with Journeymen's Union
Sperry Mfg. Co., Carriage Hardware, Ansonia, Conn.	1886-88	- -	"No perceptible benefit."
Boston Herald, Boston, Mass.	1887-88	300	Change in firm

1 Adapted from Gilman, Nicholas P., Profit Sharing Between Employer and Employee, pp. 362-3.

Table II shows that most of these plans were of extremely short duration, with the longest program, that of the A. S. Cameron and Company, being pursued for only eight years. It is also apparent that better relations did not automatically ensue when profit sharing was introduced. Four plans during this

period were specifically suspended because of strikes or trouble
with the union.

The efforts of some employers were more successful, however,
and in the Eighties, increased attention was given to profit
sharing arrangements. Table III summarizes the information
concerning the profit sharing programs of some twenty-six
companies, all of which had been introduced prior to 1889 and
were still in operation by that date.[34]

Table III[1]

Name of Establishment, Place and Nature of Business	Date	Number of Employees	Compensation
Peacedale (R.I.) Mfg. Co., Woolens	1878	450	One-half net profit
Staats-Zeitung, New York	1880	139	10 percent on wages
The Century Co., Publishers, New York	1881	- -	Dividend on certain part of stock
Pillsbury Flour Mills, Minneapolis, Minn.	1882	400	Fixed percent not published
N. O. Nelson Mfg. Co., Brass Goods, St. Louis	1886	250	Equal dividend to labor and capital
Rogers, Peet & Co., Clothiers, New York	1886	275	Fixed percent not published
Ara Cushman Co., Boot and Shoe Mfrs., Auburn, Me.	1886	650	Proportion of wages to sales
Wardwell Needle Co., Lake Village, N. H.	1886	16 to 20	50 percent
W. E. Fette, Agent for gas works, Boston, Mass.	1886	- -	Fixed percent of dividend

34 This figure is exclusive of The Riverside Press of Cambridge
which began a system of paying extra interest on savings in
1872 and the Rand, McNally Company of Chicago which started
to pay a stock dividend to chief employees in 1879.

Table III (continued)

Name of Establishment, Place and Nature of Business	Date	Number of Employees	Compensation
Hoffman & Billings Co., Brass Goods, Milwaukee	1886	- -	Equal dividend on wages and capital
E. R. Hull & Co., Clothiers, Cleveland, O.	1886	50	Definite percent of profits
Globe Tobacco Co., Detroit, Mich.	1886	- -	1 percent on sales
H. K. Porter & Co., Pittsburgh, Light Locomotives	1886	- -	- - - - - - - - -
Rumford Chemical Works, Providence, R. I.	1886	- -	- - - - - - - - -
Springfield (Mass.) Foundry Co.	1887	50	Fixed percent not published
Rice & Griffin Mfg. Co., Mouldings, Worchester	1887	75	Proportion of payroll to capital
Norriton Woolen Mills, Norristown, Pa.	1887	- -	5 percent on wages
Haines, Jones & Cadbury, Brass Goods, Phila.	1887	250	Equal dividend to labor and capital
St. Louis (Mo.) Shovel Co.	1887	100	- - - - - - - - -
S. Crump Label Co., Montclair, N. J.	1887	- -	Earnings on 10 percent on capital
Page Belting Co., Concord, N. H.	1887	- -	Earnings over 10 percent on capital
John Wanamaker, Dry Goods, etc., Phila.	1887	3000	Fixed sum not published
Yale & Towne Mfg. Co., Locks, cranes, Stamford, Conn.	1887	- -	Percent on gain made in productivity
Proctor & Gamble, Soap & candles, Ivorydale, O.	1887	400	Proportion of wages to sales
Meyer Bros., Wholesale druggists, St. Louis, Mo.	1888	200	Dividend over 6 percent on certain amt of capital
Scott & Holstein, Lumber, Duluth, Minn.	1888	30 participating	- - - - - - - - -

1 Compiled from Gilman, Nicholas P., Profit Sharing Between Employer and Employee, pp. 386-87.

Only the Peacedale Manufacturing Company had started its program

before 1880. Three others were inaugurated before 1885; ten in

1886, and twelve in the years 1887 and 1888. The largest establishment in which profit sharing was in operation by 1889 was the John Wanamaker Store, Philadelphia and, on the basis of the information presented, the smallest company to engage in this activity was the Wardwell Needle Company. The proportion of profits paid out to employees under these plans varied considerably and the method of computing their share was equally diversified. One of the companies for which this information was divulged, divided the net profits equally between labor and capital. Three companies paid equal dividends to labor and capital. In all cases, the employees were paid their share in cash, and only the Page Belting Company of Concord, New Hampshire and the John Wanamaker Store paid varying amounts to individuals in a given job based on the performance throughout the year.

Ten years later in 1899, Nicholas P. Gilman, in a similar study, reported that eight of the twenty-six successful plans in existence in 1889 were still in effect.[35] In addition to these, however, thirteen additional companies had adopted the idea. Table IV presents the twenty-one companies having profit sharing plans in 1899 and the date the program was started.

---

35 Gilman, Nicholas P., A Dividend to Labor, p. 346. In 1896, Mr. Paul Monroe reported that fifty experiments in profit sharing had been conducted in the United States up to that year. Of these, he stated that thirty-three had been permanently and five indefinitely abandoned, leaving only twelve plans in operation at that date. (Reported in Adams, Thomas S., and Sumner, Helen L., op. cit., p. 359.)

Table IV

Profit Sharing Plans in Operation in 1899[1]

Name of Establishment	Date	Nature of Business
Peacedale (R. I.) Mfg. Co	1878	Woolens
The Century Company, New York	1881	Publishers
Pillsbury Flour Mills, Minneapolis, Minn.	1882	Milling
H. K. Porter & Co., Pittsburgh	1886	Light Locomotive
N. O. Nelson Manufacturing Co.	1886	Brass Goods
Rumford Chemical Works, Providence, R. I.	1886	Chemicals
Rice and Griffin Mfg. Co., Worcester	1887	Mouldings
Proctor and Gamble Co., Cincinnati	1887	Soaps
Bourne Mills, Fall River	1889	Cotton
P. N. Kuss, San Francisco	1890	Painter
Public Ledger, Philadelphia	1890	Newspaper
Solvay Process Co., Syracuse, N. Y.	1890	Soda Ash
Ballard and Ballard Co., Louisville, Ky.	1892	Flour Mills
Acme Sucker Rod Co., Toledo, Ohio	1895	- - - - - -
Columbus (Ohio) Gas Company	1895	Utility
Broadway Central Hotel, New York	1897	Hotel
The Hub Clothing Store, Chicago, Ill.	1897	Store
The Roycroft Press, East Aurora, N. Y.	1897	Printing
South Carolina Savings Bank, Charleston	1897	Bank
Baker Mfg. Co., Evansville, Wis.	1898	Windmills
Columbus (Ohio) Traction Company	1899	Public Utility

1 Compiled from information presented in Gilman, Nicholas P., A Dividend to Labor, pp. 377-8.

It seems significant that there were fewer profit sharing plans in operation in 1899 than existed ten years earlier. An important reason for the high death rate and slow advance of such plans was the severe depression of the nineties. Nicholas P. Gilman writes: "A number of experiments in profit sharing begun not long before the protracted siege of 'hard times' (1893-1897) came to an end because of inability to earn a bonus and consequent discouragement, while others begun after the crisis had fairly set in were dropped."[36] This statement is borne out by the experience of the S. D. Warren Company, the Hofmann & Billings Manufacturing Company of Milwaukee, and the Ames Shovel and Tool Company of St. Louis. In all three cases, the employees enthusiastically endorsed profit sharing when there were profits to divide, but lost interest in it in years in which there were none.[37] Economic conditions were not the sole reason for the failures. One plan was abandoned because the employer did not approve of the use to which his employees put their share of the profits. In discussing profit sharing before the Conference on Welfare Work in 1904, Dr. Frank Parsons said:[38]

> John Wanamaker told me of the effort that he
> made in his store, and that he was not satisfied
> with the results. He only tried it for a couple
> of years, and said that the girls, when they got
> their $100 in addition, or whatever it was, could
> not be persuaded, in all cases, to save that
> money. One girl spent her money for a silk dress,

---

36 ibid., p. 348. There was also a mild depression beginning about 1907 and lasting through 1908.
37 Tolman, William H., Social Engineering, p. 206.
38 Statement before the Conference on Welfare Work, National Civic Federation in 1904.

and another for a piano, and he was not satis-
fied that they knew how to handle the money,
and that he would have to discontinue the
plan.

Because many of these plans were unable to survive, the Association for the Promotion of Profit Sharing which was formed in
1892 never became very active and soon disappeared.[39]

In 1905, Adams and Sumner found only fourteen establishments with profit sharing plans in operation.[40] All of these
plans provided for distribution of profits to wage earners
except those of the American Smelting and Refining Company,
the Filene Department Store, and the Carolina Savings Bank.[41]
The American Smelting and Refining Company included no employees
below the grade of foreman and the other two companies confined
their programs to salaried employees. There is reason to believe,
however, that restrictions on participation may have been more
prevalent. A statement made by an officer of the Solvay Process
Company, which had installed one of the most successful plans,
makes this clear:[42]

What has proved to be a successful plan of

---

39 Adams, Thomas S., and Sumner, Helen L., op. cit., p.
   359.
40 ibid. These companies were the Peacedale Manufacturing
   Company, the Columbus Railway and Light Company, the Roycroft Press, the Solvay Process Company, the Acme Sucker Rod
   Company, the Proctor and Gamble Company, the Bourne Mills,
   the Ballard and Ballard Company, the Cabot Manufacturing
   Company, the Baker Manufacturing Company the N. O. Nelson
   Company, the American Smelting and Refining Company, the Filene
   Department Store, and the Carolina Savings Bank of Charleston.
41 ibid., p. 360.
42 Statement made to the Conference on Welfare Work, National
   Civic Federation in 1904 by Mr. Louis Krumbhaar.

profit sharing was inaugurated by the board of
directors in 1887. At first only the chief
employees and general officers of the company
were admitted to participation, it being
considered that these men were in a position
to make the business of the concern more
prosperous through special care and attention,
and as an appreciation of this extra effort each
participant was allowed a certain sum, depending
upon the amount of salary he received, and the
rate of dividends allotted to stockholders; thus;
if dividends were high, the participation was
correspondingly high, and vice versa. In 1890,
the system was enlarged so as to include foremen and assistant foremen, whose participation
was based upon the foregoing method, the payments, however, being proportionately smaller.
Since the latter year the plan has been somewhat extended annually among older employees of
the classes named. The company reports that it
has reason to believe the system is an excellent
one and attains the desired end, for it has in-
cited greater interest in the affairs of the
establishment, inducing suggestions for improvements, little economies, and the exercise of
more care in consuming supplies and materials.
It has not been extended to the workmen.

On the other hand, the N. O. Nelson Manufacturing Company made
its plan applicable to all employees but inserted some rather
curious stipulations. In a letter to the Department of
Commerce and Labor in 1900, the provisions of this plan were
described:[43]

This establishment, which employs between 400
and 500 people, adopted a profit-sharing scheme
in 1886, in pursuance of which, without making
any changes in management or wages, interest
was allowed on the company's capital at 6 per

---

43 Olmstead, Victor H., op. cit.,pp. 1139-40. From 1898 to
1904 no dividends were paid either to stockholders or
employees. The plan was not abandoned, however.

cent and the remaining profits were divided
between capital and labor, after setting aside
one-tenth thereof for a reserve fund, one-tenth
for a provident fund, and one-twentieth for an
educational fund....The dividends arising under
this plan were paid in cash or in the company's
stock, according to the wish of the individual
employees, which is redeemed at par whenever
the holder for any cause leaves the service of
the company. In 1894 the rule was adopted
permitting only such employees to receive profit-
sharing dividends as saved 10 per cent of their
wages when working full time and receiving full
pay and invested it in the company's stock, the
purpose of the rule being "to offer a substantial
inducement for men when in good health and having
steady employment to save something for the future,
and also to make the sharing in the business profits
dependent on each one doing something toward it in
a direct and personal way."
    In 1892 the proportion of the profits given to
labor was increased, a 2 per cent dividend being
paid on wages to each 1 per cent on capital...

The Proctor and Gamble Company whose program was started in 1887
also shared its profits with its wage earners. The amount distributed to each employee was based on his total wages. The
dividend was computed by giving each employee the same interest
on his wage that was paid to the stockholder on his invested
capital. Thus, a worker who received $500 as an annual wage
received a dividend equal to that received by the holder of
$500 of common stock (par value) of the company.[44] A unique
variation of previously described plans was adopted by the
Columbus (Ohio) Gas Company from 1885-1895 before it switched
to a more conventional scheme. For this ten year period, the
company divided equally with its employees the saving made

44 Letter from General Manager to Department of Commerce and
    Labor dated June 22, 1899. (Reported in Olmstead, Victor H.,
    op. cit., p. 1138.)

in the cost of labor per unit of product. Thus, if a five per
cent decrease in labor cost was effected in any one year, employees received a two and one-half per cent increase in wages.
The company abandoned this plan in favor of a system similar
to the one used by the Proctor and Gamble Company in 1895
because it felt a point had been reached at which further
reduction in labor cost was not possible.[45]

The period from 1890 to 1910 witnessed many attempts to
utilize some system whereby the employee's fortunes could be
closely associated with those of the business. Employer
interest in such programs, however, was spotty. It is apparent
that no matter how carefully the program was installed or how
generous the benefits were, employee interest varied considerably
depending on whether profits were available for distribution.
By 1910, there were probably several dozen plans in operation,
but many plans had failed and by that date it was apparent that
this technique had failed to find extensive favor with employers. In 1916, the United States Department of Labor found
only 60 companies which had profit sharing plans in operation
at that time. Of these 60 companies, seven had established
their plans before 1900 and almost 50 per cent did so after
1911. Inasmuch as 50 companies had at one time or another
experimented with profit sharing plans as early as 1896, the

45 Gilman, Nicholas P., A Dividend to Labor, p. 349

death rate of such plans must have been high.

The reasons for the failure of such plans seemed to have been: (1) profit payments to employees were made annually and had little appeal until the end of the year, (2) profits were affected more by business conditions than by the efforts of the employees, and (3) the amounts distributed by many companies were too small.

Stock Purchase Plans

While many employers were trying to improve the relation-ship between themselves and their employees through profit sharing, others placed reliance upon stock purchase plans. Although the details of these plans varied, they generally permitted employees to deposit small advance payments until a sufficient sum had been accumulated to purchase a share of stock, usually common stock. Interest was usually paid on this money which was held by the company, and the stock was purchased without benefit of a discount. Sometimes, the employees could borrow money from the company to purchase stock. Table V lists the firms which had instituted some type of stock purchase plan in this period, the date the plan was started, and the nature of the business in which the company was engaged.

Table V

Companies Which Have, or Have Had, Stock Acquisition
Plans for Their Employees[1]

Name and Address of Company	Business	Date Plan Was Adopted[a]
Proctor and Gamble Company, Ivorydale, Ohio	Soaps, glycerine, and edible oils	1886
N. O. Nelson Manufacturing Co., St. Louis, Mo.	Plumbing, water works and mill supplies	1886
Illinois Central System, Chicago, Ill.	Railway Transportation	1893
Bemis Brothers Bag Company, Boston, Mass.	Cotton, jute and paper bags	1900
Pittsburgh Coal Company, Pittsburgh, Pa.	Coal	1900
Dutchess Manufacturing Co., Akron, Ohio	Men's and boys' clothing	1901
First National Bank of Chicago, Chicago, Ill.	Banking	1901
National Biscuit Company, New York, N. Y.	Bakery Products	1901
Wagner Electric Corporation, St. Louis, Mo.	Electrical Equipment	1901
Cleveland Worsted Mills Co., Cleveland. O.	Textiles	1902
Firestone Tire and Rubber Company, Akron, O.	Tires and rubber goods	1902
John B. Stetson Company, Philadelphia, Pa.	Hats	1902
Butler Brothers, Chicago, Ill.	Wholesale general merchandise	1903
Eclipse Electrotype and Engraving Co., Cleveland, O.	Printing plates and art work	1903
Leeds and Lippincott Company, Atlantic City, N. J.	Hotel operation	1903
United States Steel Corporation, New York, N. Y.	Iron and steel and their products	1903
American Stove Company, St. Louis, Mo.	Stoves	1904
International Shoe Company, St. Louis, Mo.	Shoes	1904
Ludlow Manufacturing Associates, Boston, Mass.	Jute and hemp products	1905

Table V (continued)

Name and Address of Company	Business	Date Plan Was Adopted[a]
Scruggs-Vandervoort-Barney Dry Goods Company, St. Louis, Mo.	Department Store	1905
Tracy Loan and Trust Company, Salt Lake City, Utah	Banking	1906
Boston Consolidated Gas Company, Boston, Mass.	Gas	1907
C. Howard Hunt Pen Co., Camden, N. J.	Round pointed pens	1907
Kellogg Switchboard and Supply Co., Chicago, Ill.	Telephones, switchboards, and radio equipment	1907
New Haven Gas Light Company, New Haven, Conn.	Gas	1907
Hood Rubber Company, Watertown, Mass.	Rubber tires and Footwear	1908
Ilg Electric Ventilating Company, Chicago, Ill.	Ventilating and heating apparatus	1908
Shepard Electric Crane and Hoist Company, Montour Falls, N. Y.	Cranes and hoisting machinery	1908
Bankers Trust Company, New York, N. Y.	Banking	1909
Commonwealth Edison Company, Chicago, Ill.	Electric light and power	1909
E. I. duPont deNemours & Co., Wilmington, Del.	Explosives and chemicals	1909
International Harvester Co., Chicago, Ill.	Agricultural implements	1909
Lever Brothers Company, Cambridge, Mass.	Soaps and glycerine	1909
Brooklyn Edison Company, Inc., Brooklyn, N. Y.	Light and power	1910
A. E. Nettleton Company Syracuse, N. Y.	Men's Shoes	1910
St. Albans Grain Company, St. Albans, Vt.	Poultry and dairy feed	1910

a All plans were in operation in 1910.
1 National Industrial Conference Board, Employee Stock Purchase Plans in the United States (New York: National Industrial Conference Board, Inc., 1928), p. 16.

Only five of these thirty-six companies established their programs by 1900 or earlier. Fifteen firms initiated their programs between 1901 and 1905, and sixteen between 1906 and 1910.
A distinct growth in interest in this personnel device during
this period is thus indicated. With respect to nature of the
business, the firms involved were quite diversified and no
single industry predominated. Two of the earliest endeavors
were undertaken by the N. O. Nelson Company and the Proctor
and Gamble Company in 1886. These plans, which were duplicated
by other companies in later years, permitted the employee to
secure a loan with which he might purchase the stock of the
company. In the case of the Proctor and Gamble Company, the
employee was required to furnish at least $10 and the additional
cost of the share could be borrowed from the company at four
per cent interest. Repayment of the loan was required in two
years. by 1900, some 100 employees of this company were share-
holders, owning more than 1,000 shares of stock.[46]

In May, 1893, the Illinois Central Railroad introduced
its plan which embodied a slightly different arrangement. Under
the plan, which later became fairly common, an employee could
deposit with the company sums as low as $5 for the purchase of
a share.[47] Interest was paid by the company on these deposits

---

46 Tolman, William H., Industrial Betterment (New York: The Social
    Service Press, 1900), p. 63.
47 National Industrial Conference Board, Employee Stock Purchase

and when a sufficient amount had been accumulated, the employee
received a share of stock at the prevailing market price.[48]
In December, 1900, the Pittsburgh Coal Company began selling
stock to its employees on a partial payment basis, and in the
following year, the Dutchess Manufacturing Company, a closed
corporation, gave its employees a chance to share in the disposal of some of its 8% cumulative preferred stock. Employees
of the First National Bank of Chicago, under a plan set up
that same year, were permitted to borrow from their Pension
Fund accumulations to finance partial payment subscriptions for
bank stock.[49] At the John B. Stetson Company, employees were
awarded shares on the basis of merit and length of service and
over 3,000 shares of common stock had been distributed by 1904.[50]

Stock ownership plans, like profit sharing, were subject
to fluctuating economic conditions. Moreover, participation
by employees, either by design or because of lack of interest
or funds, was limited to a small proportion of employees, there-
by weakening the effectiveness of the plan. Despite these
handicaps, stock ownership plans proved to be more popular

Plans in the United States, p. 1. Before the plan could go
into operation, however, the strike of 1894 occurred and the
proposal was dropped. It was reinstated in May, 1896.
48 Tolman, William H., Industrial Betterment, p. 65.
49 National Industrial Conference Board, op. cit., p. 1.
50 Hanger, G. W. W., op. cit., p. 1236.

than profit sharing, possibly because the objectives of such
plans were less ambitious. In addition, they required a sober-
ing financial contribution from the employee. By 1910, the idea,
although by no means universally adopted, found limited acceptance
and the foundation had been laid for more extensive growth in
later years.

Cooperative Purchasing Arrangements

Arrangements for purchasing household and other commodities
at attractive prices were established by a number of firms during
this period. Edwin L. Shuey summarizes his findings as follows:[51]

> Some companies have arrangements for purchasing
> the commodities used by their operatives at less
> than the regular retail price. For instance,
> machinist's tools that may be required, are bought
> at from ten to twenty-five percent less than they
> can be purchased at a retail store. Bicycles,
> coal and other necessities are purchased at whole-
> sale, thus saving their employes a very consider-
> able amount each year....The N. O. Nelson Company
> buys coal at wholesale rates and supplies to its
> employes at a material reduction. The Bullock
> Electrical Company assists its employes in the
> purchase of tools and bicycles. Other companies
> have arranged to assist their people to buy
> sewing machines at reduced rates.

The Illinois Steel Company promoted a plan for the cooperative
purchasing of flour, coal, potatoes, books, magazines, and
other articles. These items were bought in large quantities
by the officers of the company and sold to the employees at
wholesale prices.[52]

51 Shuey, Edwin L,, op. cit., p. 127.
52 Olmstead, Victor H., op. cit., p. 1120.

Both the Vermont Marble Company and the Plymouth Cordage
Company started several stores about 1900 so that employees
could purchase groceries and other necessities. Any profits
that were realized were distributed to employees in proportion
to their purchases.[53] The R. D. Wood Company, with a similar
program, continued to operate three stores for its employees
although they were not profitable.[54] Among the other companies
which provided this service were the National Cash Register
Company and the Lowe Brothers Company which obtained magazines,
books, and periodicals for employees at reduced prices.[55] The
Seattle Electric Company also participated by making special
arrangements with local merchants whereby employees could
purchase food, clothing, and other supplies at low prices.[56]

Pensions

The provision of income for employees upon retirement also
received consideration during this period. In 1907, the
Massachusetts legislature appointed a commission to study old
age pensions and the New Jersey Legislature did likewise in
1910.[57]

---

53 Tolman, William H., Social Engineering, p. 92.
54 ibid.
55 Shuey, Edwin L., op. cit., p. 127.
56 Tolman, William H., Social Engineering, p. 92.
57 American Association for Labor Legislation, "Review of Labor
   Legislation of 1911", American Labor Legislation Review,
   No. 3, (October, 1911), p. 121.

American railroads exhibited more interest in this type
of benefit than did industry generally. Both the Pennsylvania
and the Baltimore and Ohio Railroads instituted Pension Funds
in 1884.[58] Discussing the plan used by the Pennsylvania Railroad, Railway Age described it as a virtually original plan.
European plans studied by the company were not adaptable to
American use and there was no experience in this country to
serve as a guide.[59] Pensions for employees found favor with
other railroads and by 1908, fourteen rail systems had adopted
the idea.[60] A summary of these plans was given by the United
States Commissioner of Labor in his Twenty-Third Annual Report
in 1901:[61]

> The 14 pension systems are entirely maintained
> and controlled by the companies, the employees
> not contributing to them. The provisions of
> the systems expressly state, moreover, that no
> right to retention in the service or to a
> pension allowance is conferred. Twelve of the
> systems were instituted in the period 1900-

---

58 Gilman, Nicholas P., A Dividend to Labor, p. 274.
59 Shuey, Edwin L., op. cit., p. 121.
60 United States Commissioner of Labor, "Workmen's Insurance
   and Benefit Funds in the United States", Twenty-Third
   Annual Report, 1909, p. 274. Tolman in Social Engineering,
   (p. 176) reported that 15 railroads had pensions, namely,
   Atchison, Topeka & Santa Fe; Atlantic Coast Line; Baltimore
   and Ohio; Bessemer & Lake Erie; Buffalo, Rochester and
   Pittsburgh; Chicago & Northwestern; Delaware, Lackawana
   and Western; Houston & Texas Central; Oregon Railroad &
   Navigation Company; Oregon Short Line; Pennsylvania;
   Philadelphia and Reading; San Antonio and Arkansas Pass;
   Southern Pacific, and Union Pacific Railroads.
61 United States Commissioner of Labor, Twenty-Third Annual
   Report, p. 274-5.

1907. The Baltimore and Ohio system, a feature
of its relief department, was the pioneer, being
instituted in 1884.
    The pensions are as a rule based on age and
length of service, monthly payments for life
being made usually on the basis of 1 per cent of
the average monthly pay for the ten years next
preceding retirement for each year of service.
The majority of the companies put aside, annually,
a stated sum for pension allowances and provide
for ratable reductions in the payments whenever
the total expenditures exceed that sum.
    In most of the systems pensions for superannu-
ation are granted to employees retired at 65 or
70 years of age, after from ten to thirty years
of service, and for incapacitation, to employees
from 60 to 69 years of age, with like service.
The employing companies have so restricted the age
limit for entering their service that the usual
maximum age is now 45 years. A length of service
of not less than fifteen to twenty-five years
therefore will obtain at the retirement ages.
Pensioners are usually allowed to engage in gain-
ful occupations, but may not reenter the company's
service.

There was a considerable uniformity in the railroad programs

and all were tailored closely to conform with the original

plans drawn up in 1884. The pension program was generally

administered by a committee consisting in some cases of the

President and several directors.

    The experience of industrial firms with pension plans in

this period was quite limited and not too satisfactory. The

Solvay Process Company established a Pension Fund in 1892.

Under its provisions, the company was to deposit into a pension

fund ten per cent of the annual wage of each employee with at

least two year's service. The amount paid into the fund in-

creased progressively until twenty-five per cent of the annual

wage was credited to the employee. By 1895, the company had
deposited some $200,000 to the credit of employees, but dis-
continued the plan in that year after losing several legal suits
brought by employees. The existing credits, however, were
eventually paid out to those eligible to receive benefits.[62]

Several companies installed plans which were somewhat
less ambitious but also more successful than the one previously
described. John F. P. Lawton of the Gorham Manufacturing
Company discussed his company's plan before the Conference on
Welfare Work in 1904:[63]

> One other point I will mention in closing is our
> plan of pensions adopted May 1, 1903. Employees
> whose records are satisfactory to the company will,
> if disqualified for work on account of age or
> permanent ill health, be eligible to pensions under
> the following age limits and terms of service:
>   70 years of age, 25 years' continuous service
>   65 years of age, 35 years' continuous service
>   60 years of age, 40 years' continuous service
> When the company shall have been satisfied that an
> employee is entitled to a pension, they will cause
> the name of such employee to be placed upon the
> pension roll, and he will be paid monthly a sum
> equal to one per cent for each year's active
> service, computed at the wage paid at the time of
> enrolment, provided that no pension shall exceed
> one thousand dollars yearly.

At the same convention E. A. Stedman, Manager of the Atlantic
Department of the Wells-Fargo Company, summarized his company's
pension plan: "We have one, adopted two years ago, under
which we allow a man for each year of service one percent,

62 Olmstead, Victor H., op. cit., p. 1146.
63 National Civic Federation, Conference on Welfare Work,
   op. cit., p. 101.

of his average salary during the last ten years of his service
with the company. For instance, if a man has been with us
twenty-five years, he gets twenty-five percent of his average
salary during the last ten years, when he retires."[64] The
pension plan of the Proctor and Gamble Company, established
before 1900, provided that any employee with ten years' service,
when disabled for any cause, was entitled to a pension of 75
per cent of his average wage during the last year of employment.
A fund was created to which both the company and employee contributed, the latter usually drawing on his profit sharing
dividends.[65] Another program started by the American Steel
and Wire Company in January, 1902 was also successful. The
pension fund was maintained entirely by the company and eligbil-
ity requirements were similar to those of the Proctor and
Gamble Company. By 1909 there were 419 pensioners who received,
in that year, a total of $56,712.[66]

It is apparent that company pensions made some headway
during this period. Acceptance of this personnel device was
most pronounced in the railroad industry. Apparently the
difficulties growing out of a failure to fund plans of this

---

64 ibid., p. 134.
65 Olmstead, Victor H., op. cit., p. 1138.
66 Beyer, David S., "Safety Provisions in the United States
   Steel Corporation", The Survey, XXIV, (September, 1910),
   p. 236. Among the other companies having pension plans were
   the First National Bank of Chicago whose plan was started
   on May 1, 1899 and the National City Bank of New York which
   started its pension plan about 1897.

nature and to place them on an actuarial basis had not arisen during this period.

Insurance

The practice of providing life insurance for employees was inititated at the close of the nineteenth century. On January 1, 1899, the Siegel-Cooper Company department store presented a life insurance policy of $1,000 to some 504 men who had been employed with the company for at least a year.[67] The John B. Stetson Company also provided life insurance as a reward for service with the company, and, by 1904, was paying premiums on eighteen policies taken out for employees.[68] These were extremely isolated cases and only applied to a few people in the company. The first group life insurance policy for employees was not issued until 1911. In that year, the Pantasate Company took out insurance on its 100 employees and, in 1912, Montgomery Ward and Company also purchased group insurance for its employees.[69]

Building and Loan Associations

Building and loan associations, operating independently of industrial enterprises, were quite common throughout this period. In 1902-1903, for example, there were in the United States 5,299 of these associations with a membership of 1,530,707

---

67 Gilman, Nicholas P., A Dividend to Labor, p. 294.
68 Hanger, G. W. W., op. cit., p. 1238.
69 Dermody, Harold, Financial Aids to Employees,(Unpublished Master's Thesis, Northwestern University, School of Commerce, 1940).

and total assets of $577,228,014.[70] As a means of encouraging
home ownership and often to discourage labor turnover, a handful of industrial firms introduced similar programs of their
own devising. Typical of the plans in effect was that of the
Proctor and Gamble Company:[71]

> A Building Association was incorporated in August,
> 1887, with an authorized capital of $500,000. It
> is conducted by a board of nine directors, all
> employees of the Proctor and Gamble Company, and
> elected by the share holders of the Building
> Association. There are now 450 share holders,
> 390 of whom are simply depositors, the other sixty
> being borrowers upon real estate security. Of
> these sixty, thirty are employees of the company,
> who are paying for their homes in the association.
> It is estimated that since the incorporation of
> the association there have been sixty of the
> employees of the company that have obtained homes
> through its agency. There is $1500 in the reserve
> fund, as security against contingent losses, of
> which in the history of this association there have
> been none. Some of the members of the association,
> employees of the Proctor and Gamble Company have
> as much as $2,000 deposited to their credit. Many
> others use the association to accumulate savings,
> in order to pay for stock of the Proctor and
> Gamble Company, which they have bought and are
> paying for by installments.

One of the earliest of such plans was established by the
John B. Stetson Company in 1879. In order to encourage skilled
hatters to stay with the company, a building and loan association was created where funds could be borrowed at a low
rate of interest for the building of homes.[72]

---

70 Adams, Thomas S., and Sumner, Helen L., op. cit., p. 393.
71 Tolman, William H., Industrial Betterment, p. 64.
72 Shuey, Edwin L., op. cit., p. 137.

As an additional feature, shares in this association were offered
to employees as a reward for efficient service. By 1903, some
sixty-two people had bought homes under this plan.[73] The
Stillwell-Bierce and Smith-Vaille Company of Dayton, Ohio and
the Baltimore and Ohio Railroad had also established building
and loan associations for their employees before 1900, while
the Gorham Manufacturing Company made arrangements for employees
to borrow money from the local bank for home building purposes.[74]

Savings Plans

As part of a widespread effort to encourage workers to
save, companies introduced a number of thrift and savings
arrangements. One approach was the establishment of benefit
or thrift associations which obligated members ot lay aside a
certain sum of money each week or month. In some cases, the
firm added to this sum and paid a nominal interest on the amount
deposited. Usually the program was managed by officers of the
company and frequently an employee representative participated
in its administration. "Penny Provident" banks were also distributed to encourage children and adults to save coins.

The Ludlow Manufacturing Company established a savings
bank in 1888 which was administered by a company clerk and a
master mechanic representing the employees. The Gorham

---

73 Hanger, G. W. W., op. cit., p. 1235.
74 National Civic Federation, Conference on Welfare Work,
    op. cit., p. 101.

Manufacturing Company, the Strawbridge and Clothier Department
Store, and the Larkin Soap Company established a savings department or bank about 1899. The last-mentioned company received
deposits from employees and paid interest at the rate of five
per cent, compounded quarterly, a rate which was considerably
higher than that paid by any of the Buffalo banks. By 1903,
about one-third of the employees were depositors.[75] Interest
rates paid by companies varied considerably, with the Endicott
Johnson Company paying as high as six per cent under its plan
and the Pelzer Manufacturing Company paying only one per cent.[76]
A spokesman for the Curtis Publishing Company explained some of
the essential features of that company's program before the
Conference on Welfare Work in 1904:[77]

> The Savings Fund Society was organized several
> years ago to encourage thrift and the habit of
> saving. The sum of twenty-five cents per week
> is paid into the fund for each share and no
> person can hold more than twenty shares, making
> twenty-five cents the smallest amount per week
> and five dollars the largest amount per week
> that will be received. Each series begins on
> September 1 and ends on August 31, when a new
> series is immediately opened. An opportunity
> for a permanent investment of the money will
> then be offered by the firm. Six per cent is
> guaranteed on the savings, and last year the
> company donated to the Savings Fund the fines
> for lateness during the year, amounting to
> $450, making the interest that year eleven per
> cent. Withdrawal from the Society before the
> end of the year forfeits all interest. At any

75 Stevens, George A., and Hatch, Leonard W., op. cit., p. 233.
76 Hanger, G. W. W., op. cit., p. 1126.
77 National Civic Federation, Conference on Welfare Work,
   op. cit., pp. 165-6.

> time loans will be made for a period of not less
> than a month, and for a sum not exceeding nine-
> tenths of the amount paid in, and the rate of
> six per cent per annum. A charge of ten cents
> is made for each loan. We consider that this
> Saving Fund has been very successful.

Both the John B.Stetson Company and the Baltimore and Ohio
Railroad operated their savings programs in conjunction with the
building and loan association. In the latter concern, deposits
of employees in the savings bank were lent to the building and
loan association at six per cent. Repayment could then be
made in monthly installments through payroll deductions.[78]
Loans to employees for any purpose were made by the Cassidy
& Son Manufacturing Company of New York. No interest was charged
and the borrower repaid the loan in weekly installments of $1
until the debt was cancelled.[79]

Suggestion Systems

The system of rewarding employees for suggestions which
resulted in savings or improvements originated about 1897
with the National Cash Register Company.[80] In the first year,
employees made some 4,000 suggestions of which 1,078 were
adopted.[81] The use of cash rewards as an incentive to secure
improvements appealed to employers and by 1900, this technique
was rather widely heralded. Edwin L. Shuey described the
method for soliciting suggestions:[82]

---

78 Gilman, Nicholas P., A Dividend to Labor, p. 274.
79 Stevens, George A., and Hatch, Leonard W., op. cit., p. 108.
80 Shuey, Edwin L., op. cit., p. 91.
81 Gilman, Nicholas P., A Dividend to Labor, p. 229.
82 Shuey, Edwin L., op. cit., p. 92.

> ...autographic registers are placed in every
> department, on which the suggestor writes what
> he has to say, the register itself making a
> duplicate copy. The original is torn off and
> kept by the writer, while the duplicate is
> locked within the register. In some factories,
> a small box is used into which the employe may
> drop his written suggestion at any time. In
> still other cases, a box is supplied with a
> tablet of paper hanging by its side ready for
> use. In some cases only one box is used
> stationed near the office. In others, a box
> is placed in each of the buildings of the
> factory.
>   The suggestions having been made, the
> secretary of the Factory Committee, or some
> person appointed for the purpose, gathers those
> written statements and examines them. In every
> case, the receipt of the suggestion is im-
> mediately acknowledged and the thanks of the
> company expressed for the interest of the
> employe.

This system was deemed necessary because foremen would frequently
decline to accept suggestions or utilized them to their own
advantage.

The National Cash Register Plan became the pattern after
which most other systems were modeled. Careful thought preceded
its inauguration as is evident from the following account:[83]

> When it was determined by its originators to
> adopt this idea of suggestions, a meeting was
> called of the employes and the whole plan
> explained fully to them. This avoided, at the
> very beginning, objections and difficulties that
> might be aroused in the minds of the employes
> themselves, by showing that the purpose of the
> company was to encourage the employe and to give
> him a fair opportunity rather than to bring any
> special advantage to itself. Following this,
> printed bulletins were posted in every depart-
> ment of the factory announcing the prizes, the

---

83 ibid.

amounts, the time for competition and the methods
of examination, these bulletins being prominently
placed before the employes as a daily reminder of
their opportunities. The scope of suggestions
in almost all cases includes methods of management, improvement in tools, cheapening the form
of handling of work, changes in appearance of
buildings or grounds, or any other items of
interest or practical value for the business or
for the comfort or the help of the employes. In
every case, the offer of prizes for suggestions
is open to all employes except heads of departments and their first assistants, or those employed on regular salaries.

Employees were required to submit their suggestions in writing

to the Factory Committee using the autographic registers pro-

vided for such purpose. They could also be sent by messenger,

mail, or left with the doorkeeper.[84] The company set aside

$615. every six months to be awarded to persons submitting the

best fifty suggestions. The prize money was distributed as

follows: First Prize - $50; Second Prize - $40; Third Prize -

$30; Fourth Prize - $25; and Fifth Prize - $20. In addition,

there were fifteen prizes of $15, fifteen prizes of $10, and

fifteen prizes of $5 each.[85] These prizes were awarded at an

outdoor festival in the summer and in the Dayton Opera House

at an appropriate ceremony in the winter.[86]

The A. B. Chase Company of Norwalk, Ohio envisioned

their suggestion system as a real means for bettering the

conditions of their workers. This was evident from the initial

announcement of the program to the employees in 1889, an excerpt

---

84 Tolman, William H., Industrial Betterment, p. 13.
85 ibid., p. 12.
86 Gilman, Nicholas P., A Dividend to Labor, p. 229.

of which read:[87]

> From time to time certain suggestions are made
> by employees to the management of this company,
> which they wish to take up and adjust. The
> Company is glad to receive suggestions or
> complaints from the employees; it will be glad
> to investigate and adjust any that it can. For
> this purpose we have placed these small boxes
> around the factory; and if any employee has
> any suggestion to make we shall be glad to have
> him write it on paper and place it in these
> boxes. The employee can suit himself about
> signing his name, but we would much prefer it,
> and the superintendent will treat all such
> communications with perfect confidence, and
> will guarantee that any such will not work to
> the detriment of the employee, and in most cases
> will probably work to his advantage. It is
> the desire of this Company to have the good
> will of all the employees, and it wishes to
> adjust all matters to their satisfaction as
> far as possible.

Total cash rewards of $100 in gold were paid every six months

for the better suggestions. The first prize was $50; second

prize, $20; third and fourth prizes, $10 each, and fifth and

sixth prizes, $5 each. These were awarded at the annual picnic

in the summer and at the annual ball of the beneficial asso-

ciation in the winter.[88]

Beginning in 1899, the Cincinnati Milling Machine Company

set aside $500 annually as prizes for suggestions which resulted

in savings or improvements.[89] The Bausch and Lomb Optical

Company of Rochester also started its program in May, 1899.

Each quarter, seven prizes, varying in size from $5 to $25,

---

87 Tolman, William H., Industrial Betterment, p. 13.
88 ibid.
89 Gilman, Nicholas P., A Dividend to Labor, p. 234.

were offered for worthwhile suggestions and a grand prize of
$100 for the most valuable suggestion of the year. In less
than a month, the company had received about forty-six suggestions, some of which resulted in substantial savings.[90]
Typical of the companies which used simple suggestion boxes
were the Natural Food Company and the Curtis Publishing
Company. Cash prizes were paid at the former company for useful
ideas and, in the latter company, an advisory committee met with
the welfare manager and reviewed all suggestions and complaints.[91]
At Filene's and Sons Department Store in Boston, a suggestion
committee, which was elected by the association, had the power
to accept or reject suggestions. Prizes of $1.50 were paid for
ideas deemed acceptable by this committee.[92]

Among other companies which had adopted a suggestion
system were: the Acme White Lead Works, the J. C. Ayer Company,
the F. H. Brownell Company, the Chandler-Taylor Company of
Indianapolis, the Farrand & Votey Organ Company of Detroit,
the T. B. Laycock Company, the Parry Manufacturing Company,
the Purina Mills, the Remington-Sholes Company, the Russell
and Erwin Manufacturing Company, the Stillwell-Bierce and
Smith-Vaille Company of Dayton, Ohio, the United States Printing
Company, the Westinghouse Electric and Manufacturing Company,

90 ibid., p. 293.
91 National Civic Federation, Conference on Welfare Work,
   op. cit., p. 157-165.
92 ibid., p. 33.

and the J. H. Williams Company.

In general, companies recognized that both employer and
employees stood to benefit when profitable suggestions were
accepted and rewarded. Because results from the operation of
this program were often immediate and tangible, this personnel
activity received favorable attention. One enthusiastic
employer, after installing his program, described the results
in the following glowing terms:[93]

> Suggestions began to pour in by the hundreds.
> A glaring searchlight of criticism was turned
> upon every least fault in the operation of
> the factory. No imperfection could exist long
> where hundreds of pairs of trained eyes were
> eagerly looking for it....In the next few years
> thousands of valuable suggestions were adopted.
> A new force had been added to the company's
> powers. With its several thousand-mind power
> plant the organization forged irresistibly
> ahead.

Conclusion

The twenty-year period under study disclosed considerable
experimentation with wage incentive plans and with a number of
supplementary wage programs or employee benefits. Some of
them, such as incentive wage plans, were introduced to stimulate
productivity and to reward employees for extra effort. Profit
sharing was established in part to bring about better employee-
employer relations, but also with the hope that efficiency would
be improved and costs reduced. Most of these programs were
undoubtedly introduced for a variety of reasons. In some

93 Holman, Worthington C., "A 5,000 Brain Power Organization",
System, VI, No. 1, (July, 1904), p. 107.

cases, they were viewed as a positive approach to better
relations between the managements and their employees. Sometimes, humanitarian considerations were important. In other
cases, the desire to keep labor turnover low was a factor.
In still other instances, the company hoped to arouse employee
interest in the success of the business. No doubt the desire
for efficiency and lower costs was a predominant motive.

Many of these programs and devices, modified to meet
present-day conditions, are essential elements of personnel
administration today and all of them may be found in at least
some companies. Some of them, such as incentive wage systems,
life insurance, thrift plans, and, to a lesser extent, pension
plans have achieved fairly wide acceptance. On the other hand,
profit sharing failed to win many adherents over the years.
Throughout the period studied, the programs were initiated by
management and, with some exceptions, administered by it.

CHAPTER VI

SELECTION, TRAINING, SAFETY, AND MEDICAL WORK

In this chapter are brought together the remaining
activities and programs which today are associated with the term
personnel administration or personnel management. In this group
of activities fall selection, training and education, and safety
and medical work.

Selection

Writing in System in 1905, Herbert J. Hapgood commented:[1]

Man hunting is becoming a broad and vital work; and
it is becoming a common work. For not only are
those engaged in it who make this their sole work--
employment experts and agencies--but every large
corporation, every school which turns men and
women out into the working world, labor unions that
have men to place, employers' associations having
places to fill--all these are developing more or
less complete and independent departments for
hunting the right men or supplying the right men.

The information available for this period does not support this
enthusiastic observation. Certainly as far as industry was
concerned, there were few centralized employment departments.
Moreover, little discussion of employment policies and procedures
were uncovered in the literature of the period. Only toward the
end of the first decade of the twentieth century did firms single
out this function for special treatment. As a general rule,
the selection function in the larger companies was carried out

---

1 Hapgood, Herbert J., "How To Secure Right Men", System, VII,
No. 1, (January, 1905), p. 64.

by the line officers and in smaller organizations, the chief
executive assumed the task of hiring. In larger organizations,
it was frequently delegated to lower level supervisors. The
centralization of the employment function and the development
of more effective ways of hiring did not receive significant
attention until World War I when immigration virtually ceased
and labor became very scarce.[2]

About 1899, the B. F. Goodrich Company organized what
is considered to be the first employment department. "This
Department was known as the Employment Bureau, and its function
was and always has been the hiring of employees for the company,
with the things necessarily incident to pure hiring. Mr. Schwartz
was known as the Manager of the Employment Bureau, not as Employment Manager, and this was before the mechanics or the technique
of employment was invented or known."[3] The Westinghouse Electric
and Manufacturing Company at East Pittsburgh also organized
an employment department about this time.[4] In 1910, Meyer Bloom-
field organized the first local association of employment managers
in Boston, but the scope of activity of this group was broader
than employment alone since it placed considerable emphasis upon

2 Douglas, Paul H.,"Plant Administration of Labor", Journal of
  Political Economy, XXVII, No. 7, (July, 1919) p. 544.
3 National Association of Employment Managers, Proceedings, First
  Annual Convention (Newark: C. Wolber Company, May, 1919),
  p. 13. (From a statement made by Mr. Dudley Kennedy.)
4 National Civic Federation, Conference on Welfare Work, Proceedings (New York: Andrew H. Kellogg Co., 1904), p. 179.

vocational guidance.[5]

The first public employment office was created by the State of Ohio as early as 1890 and by 1915 some twenty-three states had established similar offices in eighty cities. These facilities were not used extensively by industrial employers.[6] Private employment agencies existed also but in many cases their motives were suspect. The amount of business done by such agencies was very small.[7]

Selection Techniques

The value of proper selection techniques was recognized in isolated instances but prevailing techniques appear crude and unrefined in light of modern methods of hiring. After 1900, the literature includes articles on the importance of selection, selection techniques and forms, including the use of an application blank, interviews, and references. In 1904, C. M. Jones wrote:[8]

> The hiring of the employe is the first point of
> contact between him and his employer, and to the

---

5 National Association of Employment Managers, First Annual
   Convention, op. cit., p. 5. In the literature of later years,
   "Employment Management", was used to refer to all industrial
   relations activities.
6 Commission on Industrial Relations, Final Report (Washington:
   Barnard and Miller Print, 1915), p. 177. The Committee reported one of the major reasons for lack of interest was
   attributable to the grave inefficiencies of many of these offices.
7 ibid., p. 176.
8 Jones, C. M., "The Employer and the Employee", System, V,
   No. 5, (May, 1904), p. 349. See also Hapgood, Herbert J.,
   "Engaging an Employee", System, V, No. 1, (January, 1904),
   pp. 86-89; and Woods, C. E., "Organizing a Factory", System,
   VI, No. 1, (July, 1904), pp. 108-112.

latter it is a matter most vital and far-reaching.
Upon the hiring of the right workmen more than on
any other one point depends the efficiency of a
working force, especially when these are unskilled
laborers. A good employee can be trained and developed up to almost any plane; a poor workman is
always a sore spot.

Selection techniques, however, were not generally in use
and most articles discussing their use frequently ended with a
plea for greater acceptance. Armour and Company had worked
out a system for the selection of office employees. Phillip
D. Armour personally interviewed each applicant. This company
did not regard the selection of factory workers as an important
function. One of the executives stated that "the employees in
the plant do not need to be hired so carefully. The common
workmen are hired and discharged by the carload."[9]

Harlow N. Higinbotham, President of the National Grocery
Company, described the method of selection he favored in the
following words:[10]

I would first look into the home conditions of an
applicant. If the applicant is a boy, I would
inquire whether he lived with his parents; this
would be in his favor. If he is a country boy
he may live with a relative, but if he lives at a
cheap boarding house it is against him, for it
may undermine his health in after life. If a boy
came to me seeking employment and owned that he
used cigarettes I would tell him to go and stop
it---not to stop when he entered my employ, but
before ever applying. This is only one incident
showing how the general health of the employe is
considered, when he is first selected. His education and general adaptability are the last to
be considered.

9 Zimmerman, T. J., "The System of the Armour's", System, V,
   No. 4, (April, 1904), p. 244.
10 Higinbotham, Harlow N., "How To Secure Employees' Loyalty",
   System, VIII, No. 7 (July, 1905), p. 26.

The attitude and approach to hiring described above appears to
have been typical of employers in this area.

Promotions

Systematic promotion as part of an overall personnel program apparently received little, if any, attention. The ex-
plicit purpose of some training programs was to prepare people
for promotion, and a few companies seemed to grasp the importance
of fair promotional policies. The Tide Water Oil Company, for
example, announced that its policy would be to promote men from
the ranks to supervisory positions.[11] Seniority was undoubtedly
an important factor governing promotions and individual supervisors exercised a great deal of influence over the promotions
of their people.[12]

Training and Education

As the nineteenth century drew to a close, employers were
beginning to experience some difficulty in finding skilled
workmen to satisfy their ever-expanding needs. Thsi problem,
which became critical during World War I, led to the introduction
of apprentice training programs after 1900. In 1909, Magnus
Alexander, a leading student of industrial problems, wrote:
"The recent period of unprecedented industrial prosperity has

11 Tolman, William H., Social Engineering (New York: McGraw-
   Hill Book Co., 1909), p. 37.
12 Gairns, J. F., "The Promotion of Employees", Cassier's Magazine, XXXII, No. 5 (September, 1907), p. 420.

revealed in a striking manner to the American people that the
supply of skilled workmen in this country is utterly inadequate....Thoughtful and far-sighted men should, therefore,
give close and careful consideration to this matter in order to
avoid a future check on the industrial development of the
country."[13] As a testimony of the concern over the inadequacy
or training, the National Society for the Promotion of Industrial
Training was founded in November, 1906. The purpose of this group
was to assist in marshalling public opinion in favor of a public
educational system that would train young boys and girls to
assume responsible positions in the factory. Other groups which
expressed alarm over the lack of training facilities included
the American Federation of Labor, the National Association of
Manufacturers, the National Education Association, the National
League for Industrial Education, the Southern Industrial Education Association, the National Metal Trades Association, the
International Typographical Union, and the Young Men's Christian
Association.[14] In addition to the interest manifested by private
groups, governmental bodies at the state and municipal levels
were directing their attention to this matter. By 1909, seven
states had created commissions by legislative enactment to

---

13 Alexander, Magnus W., "The Apprenticeship System of the General
   Electric Company at West Lynn, Massachusetts," The Annals,
   33, No. 1, (January, 1909), p. 141.
14 United States Commissioner of Labor, "Industrial Education,"
   Twenty-fifth Annual Report, 1910, p. 391.

conduct investigations and recommend proper measures for obtaining effectual training.[15]

Reasons for the Decline of Training

In the United States a system of apprenticeship had been
utilized until after the Civil War, when the advent of the larger
contractor brought an increase in the number of low paid "helpers"
who took the place of apprentices.[16] Employers found it more
expedient to use cheap immigrant labor for more menial jobs and
to hire skilled foreign workmen rather than train workers over
a protracted period. Changing industrial conditions, accompanied
by an influx of immigrants, thus led to a gradual decline of the
existing apprentice system.

The development of larger and more highly mechanized firms
with jobs demanding less skill was a major factor contributing to
this breakdown. The United States Commissioner of Labor stated
in his Annual Report in 1910:[17]

> The old-time apprenticeship system was never
> formally given up, but as a matter of fact it
> almost disappeared during the latter part of
> the last century. In many cases apprentices
> were not taken, and even where the name was
> still used there was a strong tendency in

---

15 ibid., p. 377. These states included Connecticut, 1903;
   Massachusetts, 1905; Maryland and New Jersey, 1908; and
   Maine, Michigan, and Wisconsin, 1909.
16 Adams, Thomas S., and Sumner, Helen L., Labor Problems (New
   York: The Macmillan Co., 1905), p. 436.
17 United States Commissioner of Labor, Twenty-Fifth Annual
   Report, p. 145.

> the interest of a large output to keep the so-
> called apprentice at one operation or on one
> machine long after he was thoroughly familiar
> with it and should have been advanced to some-
> thing else. Consequently when he had finished
> his term he might know one or two parts of his
> trade thoroughly, but he was but little better
> qualified as an all-around skilled worker than
> when he began.
> As a result of this condition employers have
> found themselves confronted with such a scarcity
> of well-trained skilled workers as to seriously
> hamper their industrial enterprises.

The great demand for skilled workmen was a temptation to half-

taught apprentices to sacrifice their trade education for an

immediate job at much higher wages. Employers, under pressure

to get out work, would assign partially-trained apprentices to

regular jobs and designate such work as constituting a part of

the training program.

The Industrial Commission of Massachusetts pointed up

another reason for the decline. "For the great majority of

children who leave school to enter employments at fourteen and

fifteen, the first three or four years are practically waste

years, so far as the productive value of the child, and so far

as increasing his industry and productive efficiency are concerned.

The employments upon which they enter demand so little individual

skill that they are not educative in any sense." The early age

at which children who were physically and mentally immature

entered industry, coupled with the fact that they had received

little manual training in the public schools, lessened their attractiveness to employers except for the most menial jobs.[18]

The practical operation of the system also weighed against
its success and growth. The education of the apprentice was
generally placed in the hands of a skilled journeyman who received
no pay for this extra work. If the latter was on piece work,
the time spent on training actually reduced his wages and, in
some cases, if the apprentice showed himself competent in his
work, he displaced his teacher at lower wages.[19]

As a result of the operation of these factors, the apprenticeship system which had been used from earliest times was no longer
extensively employed. The Twelfth Census in 1900 revealed the
low ebb to which apprentice training had fallen. This Census
showed 81,842 "apprentices" and "apprentices and helpers" in
sixteen trades and "other miscellaneous industries." Only 2.5
percent of all the persons engaged in these occupations, however,
were "apprentices" or "apprentices and helpers", the highest
proportions being 5.7 percent among the "plumbers and gas and steam
fitters", 5.9 percent among the "machinists", and 6.7 percent in
"other miscellaneous industries."[20] Some observers concluded
that private firms could not cope with the problem and they, therefore, advocated that this training be undertaken in cooperation
with the public school system.[21] A number of industrial

18 Adams, Thomas S., and Sumner, Helen L., op. cit., p. 436.
19 ibid., p. 437.
20 ibid., p. 440.
21 ibid., These writers predicted that industrial education would
   eventually supersede the apprenticeship training of private
   firms.

firms, however, launched their own training programs which were called "corporation schools." It is to a discussion of these schools that we now turn.

Apprentice Training in Manufacturing Industries

The Twenty Fifth Annual Report of the United States Commissioner of Labor dealt with existing training problems and the important contribution to be made by corporate training. A portion of this report reads as follows:[22]

> These schools are a decidedly recent development, for although one or two, notably that conducted by R. Hoe & Company, were established a generation ago, very few go further back than the beginning of the present century, and the majority have come into existence since 1905. They are an attempt on the part of manufacturers to provide a substitute for the old-time apprenticeship, which has been practically driven out by the modern emphasis on specialization and subdivision of work. Under modern conditions few or no shops offered the beginner a chance to learn more than one small part of a trade, and in consequence within the last decade manufacturers quite generally have found their operations hampered by a lack of all-round skilled workmen able to do high-grade work and to take positions as foremen, etc.

The Seventeenth Annual Report of the United States Commissioner of Labor published in 1902 had described the programs of only two companies, the Baldwin Locomotive Works and the Brown

---

22 United States Commissioner of Labor, Twenty-Fifth Annual Report, p. 20. As these schools increased in number, the National Association of Corporation Schools was formed in 1913 to provide more information for participating companies on this type of activity.

and Sharpe Company. At the close of the nineteenth century,
these two companies and the R. Hoe and Company appear to have
been the leading industrial firms which combined both shop and
school training in a formal apprentice program.[23] These programs
were cited with approval inasmuch as an opportunity was provided
for the apprentice to master a complete trade before being
assigned to his regular production job.[24] The paucity of
formal industrial training being carried on by private industry
at that time is evidenced by the fact that this report was confined almost exclusively to the work being done by trade and
technical schools.

By 1910, however, the number of companies having formal
training for apprentices had increased. In that year, the
United States Commissioner of Labor reported on the apprentice
training programs of fifteen companies. The names of these
companies and the dates that formal training was initiated are
presented in Table I.

Table I shows that only R. Hoe and Company had instituted
formal training for apprentices prior to 1900. There is a
possibility that the Brown and Sharpe Company and the International Harvester Company may also have started their programs
in the nineteenth century. Twelve of the companies originated

---

23 United States Commissioner of Labor, "Trade and Technical
   Education", Seventeenth Annual Report, 1902, p. 381.
24 ibid. The inference made is that other companies did make
   some effort to train young men on skilled jobs but that
   frequently when the apprentice demonstrated an aptitude for
   a particular type of work his training ceased.

Table I

Manufacturing Companies with Established Formal
Apprentice Training Programs, 1910[1]

Company	Date Started
R. Hoe and Company, New York	1872
Baldwin Locomotive Company, Philadelphia	1901
General Electric Company, West Lynn, Mass.	1902
Fore River Shipbuilding Company, Quincy, Mass.	1906
Westinghouse Air Brake Company, Wilmerding, Pa.	1906
Cadillac Motor Car Company, Detroit, Michigan	1907
George V. Cresson Company, Philadelphia	1907
Western Electric Company, Chicago	1907
Yale and Towne Manufacturing Company, Stamford, Conn.	1907
Lakeside Press, Chicago	1908
Solvay Process Company, Solvay, N. Y.	1908
American Locomotive Company, Dunkirk, N. Y.	1909
Westinghouse Electric & Manufacturing Co., East Pittsburgh	1909
Brown and Sharpe Company, Providence	n. a.
International Harvester Company, Chicago	n. a.

1 Compiled from the Twenty-Fifth Annual Report of the United
  States Commissioner of Labor, pp. 167-181.
n. a. Not available

their programs in the first decade of the current century. In

addition to the training programs presented in Table I, two

others had been started by 1910. In 1908, the Manufacturers'
Association of Bridgeport, Connecticut established a school for
machinists and tool-making apprentices which was operated by the
Young Men's Christian Association. The other program, the North
End Union School of Printing, was started in 1900 by the master
printers of Boston.

The training of apprentices was generally conducted in one
of three ways. Usually it was planned and managed by the company
employing the apprentices. Some companies, however, cooperated
with public schools which furnished textbook instruction and
equipment while the corporation furnished the shop instruction.
A third group utilized the services of the young Men's Christian
Association.[25]

In general, the plan of all these schools was to train the
boys in the actual work of the shop and, at the same time,
instruct them in mathematics, mechanical drawing, and other
subjects essential to the trade. Some cultural courses were
occasionally included as an incidental part of the training.
As a rule, the boy was indentured for a four-year period, although
in some cases this training was reduced to two years, Textbook
instruction was given either during regular working hours or in
evening school, at which compulsory attendance was required for

---

25 United States Commissioner of Labor, Twenty-Fifth Annual
Report, p. 166.

several hours of instruction per week. The boys were usually paid
their regular wages during school hours and upon satisfactory
completion of the course were frequently given bonuses ranging
from fifty to one hundred and fifty dollars. The students were
closely observed and the teaching was modified as much as possible
to individual needs. Usually the foreman acted as shop instructor
and sometimes the school instructor was also an employee who had
other duties about the shop.[26] Infrequently these schools were
headed by persons from the field of public education on the
assumption that they were better equipped for the training function than were line personnel. In such cases, these directors
of education, as they were called, tended to introduce classroom
formality into the program.[27]

Apprentice Training on the Railroads

The Grand Trunk Railway made the pioneering attempt to
solve the problem of a shortage of skilled labor in its shops
by establishing a school to train apprentices in 1902 at Battle
Creek, Michigan.[28] Apparently little consideration was given to

---

26 The above description is based on a summary of the nature of
corporation schools which was presented in the Twenty-Fifth
Annual Report of the United States Commissioner of Labor.
This report also describes the training programs of the
individual companies.
27 Stewart, Bryce M., Development of Industrial Relations in
the United States (New York: Industrial Relations Counselors,
Inc., 1949), p. 21.
28 United States Commissioner of Labor, Twenty-Fifth Annual
Report, p. 147.

this problem by other railroads, however, until a warning was sounded in a paper before the Railway Mechanics' Association in 1905. Soon after this warning, the New York Central Railroad and the Central Railroad of New Jersey put into operation plans to train apprentices. Thereafter, the Santa Fe; the Delaware & Hudson; the Delaware, Lackawanna & Western, and the Erie Railroad soon followed suit.[29]

There were no major differences between the apprentice training programs of the railroads and industrial firms. The programs varied in specific details, but all were directed toward producing more skilled workmen and supervisors. The apprentice generally divided his time between the shop and classroom and most railroads made every effort to secure highly competent instruction in both areas. Apprentices of the Grand Trunk Railway were required to attend classes on their own time but this was the exception and not the rule. A somewhat different approach was followed by the Southern; the Cincinnati, Hamilton & Dayton, and the Alabama Great Southern Railroads. In each of these cases, the railroad furnished the room and the equipment

---

29 ibid., p. 148. A total of 14 railroads were reported to have had apprentice training programs although not at all shops of the roads. With the exception of the programs of the New York Central Railroad and the Central Railroad of New Jersey which were established in 1905, all were started between 1907 and 1910. Railroads which had apprentice programs other than those previously mentioned were: the Pennsylvania; the Union Pacific; the Chicago Great Western; the Pere Marquette; the St. Louis & San Francisco; the Southern; the Cincinnati, Hamilton & Dayton; and the Alabama Great Southern Railroads.

and the International Correspondence School conducted the course. Apprentices were required to train at their own expense which approximated seventy-five dollars a year.[30]

Cooperative Industrial Schools

A method employed by some companies, either singly or collectively, was the use of half-time and part-time cooperative industrial schools. Under this arrangement, an employer or group of employers would agree to excuse young employees from work to attend school This system permitted training to reach a much larger number of employees and also gave smaller employers an opportunity to participate in training.

In 1910, the United States Commissioner of Labor reported on six half-time cooperative industrial schools.[31] These schools, in which the employee divided his time equally between the classroom and the shop, were founded around 1910.[32] The earliest school was started by a group of manufacturers in 1908 at Fitchburg, Massachusetts. Under this plan, which was rather typical, the candidate had to be at least fifteen years of age and had to have a grammar school education in order to qualify. The course lasted four years and each employee under the program

---

30 ibid., p. 166.
31 ibid., p. 187. These included firms cooperating with the Fitchburg High School, Fitchburg, Mass., the Beverly Independent Industrial School, Beverly, Mass.; the Technical High School, Providence; the Freeport High School, Freeport, Illinois, the Lewis Institute, Chicago, and the Cincinnati High School, Cincinnati, Ohio.
32 ibid.

was required to spend 23 hours a week for forty weeks in school.[33]

In part-time industrial cooperative schools, the pupils
attended school much less than half of the time and the instruction
was more closely correlated with shop work than was characteristic
of half-time schools. These part-time schools, which were designed
to conform more closely to the apprentice schools of private firms,
were of two general types.[34] Under one arrangement, the pupils
worked in the establishment at which they were employed but were
excused a few hours a week from shopwork to attend school. In
another type, the student was sent to school during the company's
slack season. The Twenty-fifth Annual Report of the United States
Commissioner of Labor discussed the cooperative arrangements made
with seven schools.[35] Table II summarizes this information.

The earliest school was established in Chicago, but the idea
is reported to have originated in Cincinnati.[36] As can be seen
from Table II, there was considerable variation in the requirements with respect to the number of weeks and the number of hours
per week of schoolroom instruction. However, the minimum age
for entrance was sixteen in all cases. The basic courses included
shop arithmetic, mechanical drawing, and usually some English
spelling, and elementary industrial science. The school instructor

---

33 ibid.
34 ibid., p. 199.
35 ibid.
36 ibid.

Table II

Part-time Cooperative Industrial Schools[1]

Name of School and Location	Year of estab-lishment	Years in course	Weeks of school in year	Hours of school at-tendance per week	Minimum age for entrance
Horace Mann School, Chicago, Ill.	1907	4	12	27½	16
James Otis School, Chicago, Ill.	1907	4	12	25	16
Cincinnati Continuation School, Cincinnati, O.	1909	4	48	4	16
Franklin Union, Boston, Mass.	1909	2	24	4	16
Mechanics' Institute of Rochester, Rochester, N.Y.	n. a.	3	26	4½	16
David Ranken, Jr. School of Mechanical Trades, St. Louis, Mo.	1910	2	46	7	16
State Trade School, Bridgeport, Conn.	1910	2	35	4	16

1 Adapted from the Twenty-Fifth Annual Report of the United States Commissioner of Labor, 1910, p. 199.
n. a. Not available

in some cases also coordinated the work in the school and the shop and spent a part of each week in various shops.[37]

Other Industrial Training Programs

Although apprentice training was the principal effort along

---

37 ibid.

the lines of formal industrial training, other types of training were undertaken. This training followed no particular pattern but varied rather markedly in scope and organization. One of the most elaborate educational programs was conducted by the John Wanamaker Commercial Institute at Philadelphia which was founded in 1897 to train younger store members for promotion. The younger boys and girls of the store attended classes taught by public school instructors until ten o'clock in the morning. The curriculum included many subjects which were part of the public school education. By 1909, there were 7900 graduates of the school.[38] A similar school was conducted by the Daniels and Fisher Department Store in Denver, Colorado.

The New York City Railway Company apparently introduced the first company training program for a semi-skilled occupation. Candidates for the job of motorman were trained in a special room which contained all the electric devices they would use in the operation of streetcars. According to a statement of President H. H. Vreeland, the policy was not to permit the learner on the street until he had spent at least four days in this "vestibule" school.[39]

Some companies made arrangements for evening classes on a variety of subjects. The Joliet Steel Company, for example,

---

38 Wanamaker, John, "The John Wanamaker Commercial Institute, A Store School", The Annals, 33, No. 1, (January, 1909), pp. 151-2.
39 National Civic Federation, Conference on Welfare Work, op. cit., p. 149.

made it possible for its employees to take courses in mechanical
drawing, mathematics, vocal music, penmanship, stenography, and
other subjects.[40] Filene's and Sons and the Jordan and Marsh
Department Store in Boston, on the other hand, limited their
courses to lectures on salesmanship and personality development.[41]
Among the other companies which provided evening classes for
employees were the N. O. Nelson Company, the Colorado Fuel and
Iron Company, the John B. Stetson Company, the Cleveland Window
Glass Company, the Peacedale Manufacturing Company, the Westinghouse Electric and Manufacturing Company, the Fels and Company,
the West and Simons Company, the Santa Fe Railroad, the Metropolitan Life Insurance Company, the Plymouth Cordage Company,
and the National Cash Register Company.

Brief talks after lunch was another educational technique
that was used by a number of companies. At the National Cash
Register Company, these talks were usually given by guest speak-
ers to the members of the Officers Club.[42] At the John B.
Stetson Company and the H. J. Heinz Company, a five-minute talk
was generally delivered to the employees by a member of management.[43] A quite unusual feature of the training program of

---

40 Olmstead, Victor H., "The Betterment of Industrial Conditions",
   U. S. Department of Commerce and Labor, Bulletin No. 31, (Washington: Government Printing Office, 1900), p. 1120.
41 National Civic Federation, Conference on Welfare Work, op. cit.,
   p. 31.
42 Tolman, William H., Industrial Betterment (New York: The Social
   Service Press, 1900), p. 39.
43 ibid., p. 10.

the National Cash Register Company was to send skilled workers
and their wives, at company expense, to visit industrial firms
in other cities. The first trip was made to New York in 1902
and subsequent trips were made to Philadelphia, Pittsburgh, and
other cities.[44]

Other Training Agencies
Industrial Training in Public Schools

Industrial training in public schools was practically unknown prior to 1875 and made little headway until after 1900.
The earliest experiments undertaken by public schools were conducted, with few exceptions, in institutions for dependent
children and for Indian and Negro children. Some public schools
offered evening continuation classes for apprentices and journey-
men before 1900.

Courses in day schools for pupils who might wish to enter
trades did not find much favor. There was a general feeling
that trade training was the affair of employers, not of the
general public. This feeling, coupled with a very strong
sentiment that public schools should only give cultural courses,
operated to prevent the introduction of such training.[45] An
exception was made in the case of manual training. In 1890,
according to the report of the Commissioner of Education for
1899-1900, manual training was offered by public schools in

44 ibid., p. 12.
45 United States Commissioner of Labor, Twenty-Fifth Annual
   Report, pp. 93-4.

37 cities and towns of 8,000 population or over. In 1894,
this number had increased to 95; in 1896, the number was 121,
and in 1900, it rose to 169.[46] By 1910, some of the earlier
opposition to industrial training in public schools began to
subside.[47]

Broadly speaking, there were two classes of public industrial schools -- those established by local authorities as part
of the regular public school system of cities and those organized
and conducted under a special state law and subject wholly or
in part to state control. In schools of the latter class, the
instruction was sometimes conducted in cooperation with the public
school system and in other places it operated entirely independently.[48]

By 1910, four states had established systems of industrial
education apart from the regular public school systems. New
Jersey enacted legislation in 1881 authorizing financial aid
for industrial schools. Massachusetts began to subsidize
textile schools as early as 1897, and later gave financial support
to schools offering evening instruction to workers. In 1907,
Connecticut followed with a provision for state aid for industrial
training. New York introduced similar legislation in 1908.[49]

---

46 United States Commissioner of Labor, Seventeenth Annual Report,
   p. 21.
47 United States Commissioner of Labor, Twenty-Fifth Annual
   Report, p. 94.
48 Ibid.
49 Ibid., pp. 95-106.

In addition to state-supported schools, a number of cities,
including Philadelphia, New York, Altoona, Milwaukee, Washington,
and Columbus, Ohio sponsored special schools operated in conjunction with the public school.

Correspondence School Training

One of the earliest of these schools was the International
Correspondence School of Scranton, Pennsylvania, which was founded
in 1891. Correspondence courses for occupational training were
also offered by the American School of Correspondence, Chicago
and the extension division of the University of Wisconsin. The
Educational Bureau of Information of the Union Pacific Railroad
was órganized to enable employees to take its correspondence
courses without tuition charges.[50]

Young Men's Christian Association

Educational work was conducted in about 400 different locals
of the Y. M. C. A. in 1910. In the year 1909-1910, it was estimated that these classes, talks, and lectures were attended by
330,000 employed men and boys. In that year, over 53,600
students were enrolled in some 120 subjects taught by 2,443
teachers.[51] Although these courses were not exclusively trade

---

50 ibid., p. 352. The New York Switch and Crossing Company
reimbursed employees who successfully completed correspondence
courses. (Tolman, William H., Social Engineering, p. 274).
51 ibid., p. 363.

or vocational, instruction was given in such subjects as commercial courses, mechanical drawing, and subjects which gave students
a more comprehensive and theoretical background of their trade.
Most of the courses were held at night but in a few cases they
were held during the day and, as has been previously discussed,
sometimes in cooperation with private employers.

Activities Related to Training

Vocational Guidance

It is interesting to find that vocational guidance and
counselling had received some attention in the latter part of
the period under consideration. On this subject the United
States Commissioner of Labor reported in 1910:[52]

> Vocational guidance is the newest development
> in connection with industrial education, the
> term being practically unknown and the thing
> practically nonexistent five years ago. As
> connected with industrial education it is
> based on the fact that the great majority of
> children at the time when they leave school
> and go to work have really made no choice of
> a pursuit at all, but take the first position
> they can get, regardless of its fitness to
> them or theirs to it....Vocational guidance is
> developing along many lines, but all are based
> on the fundamental idea of preventing waste of
> time and life by helping workers to choose the
> right occupation, and then to fit themselves
> thoroughly for it. The idea is gaining rapidly
> in favor, and the movement is becoming wide-
> spread.

No evidence was found to indicate that vocational guidance had
received wide acceptance in industry in the period under study.

---

52 ibid., p. 28.

Company Non-Industrial Courses

Some of the companies provided a wide variety of courses
and programs for employees, and sometimes their families, which
were unrelated to the workers' industrial training. An outstanding program of this kind was conducted by the National Cash
Register Company. It established a kindergarten for workers'
children.[53] It also fitted up a model cottage to facilitate
its instruction in proper health habits, cooking, and housekeeping to the wives of its employees. Boys were taught gardening in a special plot of ground reserved for such purpose. Employees and their families were offered lectures in which lantern
slides were used.[54] A dancing class, started in 1900, enrolled
550 members and a wood carving class was begun in 1902[55] The
Solvay Process Company also furnished non-industrial courses.[56]
In 1886, the wife of the company's president started a sewing

---

53 Tolman, William H., Industrial Betterment, p. 44. Other
   firms which helped maintain kindergartens or other public
   school facilities were the Colorado Fuel and Iron Company;
   the D. E. Sicher Company of New York; Steinway & Sons, New
   York; Astoria Silk Works Company, New York; N. O. Nelson
   Company; the Ludlow Manufacturing Company; and the Plymouth
   Cordage Company.
54 Shuey, Edwin L., Factory People and Their Employers (New
   York: Lentilhon & Co., 1900), p. 102.
55 Tolman, William H., Social Engineering, p. 276.
56 Other companies which gave some training of this nature
   included: The Natural Food Company; Warner Brothers of Bridgeport; the Ludlow Manufacturing Company; Plymouth Cordage
   Company; the Pelzer Manufacturing Company; the Roycroft Shop;
   the R. D. Wood Company; the T. B. Laycock Manufacturing
   Company; the Iron Clad Manufacturing Company; and the
   Colorado Fuel and Iron Company.

school for girls. The company also sponsored classes in household work and cooking for women. A gymnastic class for boys
and girls over twelve years of age was formed in 1887, and
later a dancing class was organized.[57] The Warner Brothers
Company of Bridgeport Connecticut offered courses in music and
literature.[58]

Company Publications

Many company publications were introduced during the
period under study. Generally speaking, the principal purpose
was to stimulate a better feeling toward the company on the
part of the employees. These magazines and papers supplied the
employees with information about the company, its history,
policies, markets, processes, and problems. They also included
special features and personal information about employees and
their families and often gave considerable publicity to the
company's personnel activities. While this material was prepared to stimulate loyalty to the organization, much of it was
educational in nature.

At least fifteen companies were known to have established
some type of company publication in this period. Of these, four
periodicals were introduced between 1892 and 1899, eight were

57 Gilman, Nicholas O., A Dividend to Labor, A Study of Employers'
   Welfare Institutions (Boston: Houghton, Mifflin and Company,
   1899), p. 286.
58 ibid., p. 263.

started in the period 1900-1904, and three were begun between 1905 and 1907. The earliest publication is believed to have been the N. C. R. which was first published by the National Cash Register Company in 1892.[59] This bi-monthly magazine was designed primarily to disseminate information about the company's many betterment activities, but also contained articles on the firm's policies on selling and manufacturing. Ten years later, the company issued Women's Welfare and in 1904, Men's Welfare and the Bulletin were added to the publication list. Factory News was introduced in 1905. These specialized publications replaced the original magazine, N. C. R.[60]

The Chameleon, a bi-monthly publication, was first issued by the Sherwin-Williams Company in 1898. This magazine consisted of company news, special features and articles written by department heads.[61] In 1899, the T. B. Laycock Manufacturing Company began to publish Factory News which was explicitly aimed at improving employee-employer understanding. William H. Tolman said of this organ: "...it has been most successful in promoting a closer and more sympathetic touch, as well as a mutual feeling of good will, between employers, officers, heads of departments, and employees."[62] The same purpose motivated the publication of Men of Monaghan started in 1904 by Monaghan Mills, Greenville,

59 Tolman, William H., Social Engineering, p. 32.
60 ibid.
61 ibid., p. 28.
62 ibid., p. 33

South Carolina, <u>Burt's Box Bulletin</u> first published by the F. N.
Burt Company, Buffalo, New York in 1903, and <u>Little Blue Flag</u>
begun by Lowe Brothers, Dayton, Ohio in April, 1901. Although
<u>Camp and Plant</u>, published by the Colorado Fuel and Iron Company,
also served this purpose, it covered a wide range of information.
Later, this publication was superseded by the <u>Bulletin, Sanitary
and Sociological</u>.[63] Portions of this later magazine were printed
in Italian, German, and other languages, The subscription price
was $1,00 per year and was apparently quite popular with employ-
ees.[64]

In several companies, the employees were assigned the responsibility for editing the newspaper or magazine. This was the
case in four large department stores including Filene's and Sons,
Strawbridge and Clothier, the Siegel-Cooper Department Store, and
Jordan Marsh and Company. <u>F. C. A. Echo</u>, published by the employees of Filene's, and <u>Thought and Work</u> by the employees of the
Siegel-Cooper Department Store, were sold for five and three
cents respectively.[65] It was not a general practice to levy a
charge for these publications.

Other companies which had made use of company publications
are the Illinois Steel Company; the First National Bank of Chicago;

---

63 ibid., p. 34.
64 Hanger, G. W. W., "Housing of the Working People in the
   United States", Department of Commerce and Labor, <u>Bulletin
   No. 54</u> (Washington: Government Printing Office, September,
   1904), p. 1200.
65 Tolman, William H., <u>Social Engineering</u>, p. 36.

Metropolitan Trust and Savings Bank, Chicago; Montgomery Ward
and Company; the H. J. Heinz Company; the F. A. Brownell Company;
Eastman Kodak; the Acme White Lead Company; Lever Brothers, and
the Stoddard Manufacturing Company.

Safety and Medical Facilities

There is much evidence to suggest that at the beginning of
this period, employers did not place a high premium on human
lives. Employers frequently operated with almost shocking indifference to industrial accidents and neither legislation nor
labor organizations were potent enough to force them to do otherwise. Prevailing common law principles, under which the burden
of proof in any industrial accident always rested with the
employee, failed to provide employers with an incentive to
establish safe conditions of work.[66] At the turn of the century,
public opinion, long disturbed over industrial accidents, began
to exert some pressure for a more humane approach. Some employers began to see that industrial accidents were costly to themselves as well as to the workers. As a result, a few medical
and safety programs emerged. Before the first decade of the

---

66 Although Maryland (in 1902) and New York (in 1910) passed
   laws to offset the employer defenses under common law doctrine,
   they were declared unconstitutional. In 1908, the federal
   government passed a compensation law covering certain of
   its employees. It was not until 1917 that the constitutionality of Workmen's Compensation laws was established by the
   United States Supreme Court. (Peterson, Florence, Survey of
   Labor Economics (New York: Harper & Brothers, 1947), p. 738.

present century had ended, safety programs and the use of medical and hospital facilities received increasing attention from employers.

Accident Prevention

Considerable public interest in the prevention of industrial accidents prevailed in this country during the closing decades of the eighteenth century. Proponents of industrial safety pushed for enabling legislation in many of the state legislatures. The Commission on Industrial Relations, appointed by President Wilson, reported in 1914, however, that only a few states had passed laws and these often covered only minor mechanical safeguards and were inadequately enforced.[67] On the other hand, Thomas I. Parkinson, writing several years earlier, stated that 22 states had enacted legislation which sought to ensure greater safety in factories.[68] The growing interest in this phase of human relations is demonstrated by the fact that by 1909, commissions had been appointed to investigate industrial accidents and suggest remedial legislation in New York, Wisconsin, and Minnesota. Workmen's Compensation laws which were to exert a marked impact on accident prevention in later years had not as yet been declared constitutional. Additional evidence of the increasing attention that was being

---

67 Commission on Industrial Relations, op. cit., p. 41.
68 Parkinson, Thomas I., American Labor Legislation Review, Vol. 1, No. 2 (June, 1911), p. 103. Thomas I. Parkinson pointed out in the January issue of that year (p. 56) that the federal government had passed legislation providing for safety appliances on railroads as early as 1893.

given to safety was a Museum of Safety Devices, patterned after
an exhibit shown in Amsterdam in 1893, which was established in
New York in 1907 and again in 1908. At the 1908 exposition,
there were 112 exhibitioners.[69]

Statistics on industrial accidents were woefully inadequate. Those that were available were very disturbing. Frederick
L. Hoffman reported that 3,000 fatal accidents occurred annually
in coal mining, and among railway trainmen, the fatal accident
rate while at work was nearly three times the normal accident
frequency among males in all occupations.[70] The increased public
agitation for legislation that would reduce industrial accidents
undoubtedly caused a growing number of companies to introduce
safety programs. The safety movement, however, did not really
get underway until the second decade of the twentieth century
when workmen's compensation laws which required employers to
pay their workers for injuries and loss of life sustained in
industrial accidents were enacted.

Safety Work at the United States Steel Corporation - One of the
earliest and certainly the most outstanding program designed to
reduce industrial accidents was launched by the United States
Steel Corporation in 1906. It is estimated that this program
cost the company $1,000,000 per year.[71] In April, 1908, a

69 Tolman, William H., Social Engineering, p. 115.
70 "Industrial Accidents and Industrial Diseases", Quarterly
   Publication, American Statistical Association, New Series,
   No. 88, (December, 1909), p. 570.
71 Morgan, Earl B., Conservation of Our Human Equipment - A

central safety committee consisting of executives responsible for
safety in the company's subsidiaries was formed.[72] Safety
committees which reported to this central committee, as well
as safety inspectors, were appointed for each plant. In two
years, from 1908 to 1910, these inspectors submitted over
6,000 recommendations to the central safety committee, ninety-
three per cent of which were adopted and carried out by the sub-
sidiary companies.[73] Although the recommendations of the inspectors and their implementation constituted the core of the
program, other devices were also utilized. Signs, for example,
were posted in conspicuous places near hazardous operations or
crossings and little safety "sermonettes" were printed on the
back of the workers' pay envelopes.[74]

Other Industrial Safety Programs - The Baldwin Locomotive Works
established a system for inspecting all machinery including
weekly examinations of cranes and elevators. In addition,
safety instructions were issued to all new employees.[75] The
Westinghouse Electric and Manufacturing Company and the J. H.
Williams Company made a real effort to place screens or guards

Dollar and Cents Proposition, paper presented before the
Executive Committee of the National Boot and Shoe Manufacturers,
Cincinnati, (April 27, 1918), p. 3.
72 Beyer, David S., "Safety Provisions in the United States
Steel Corporation:, Survey, XXIV, (September, 1910), p. 205
73 ibid., p. 206.
74 ibid., p. 229. The following is an example of these sermonettes:
"The exercise of care to prevent accidents is a duty which you
owe to yourself and your fellow employees."
75 Tolman, William H., Social Engineering, p. 112.

on elevators, crane tracks, pulleys, band saws, and other
dangerous pieces of equipment.[76] About 1904, the Solvay Process
Company inaugurated a series of lectures on "First Aid to the
Injured" which was delivered by prominent physicians. Company
guards were required to attend this course and interested employees were permitted to enroll. Those who successfully completed the course and passed an examination were given an appropriate badge to wear.[77] The Endicott-Johnson Company installed
a safety device which enabled an employee to prevent serious
accidents by pressing a button which would stop the main engine
and all machinery in the area involved.[78]

Payments to Employees for Accidents - It was not customary for
industrial firms to make payments to employees when they were
injured. A few companies, however, made such payments.[79] The
United States Steel Corporation, for example, in cases of pro-
longed disability, rendered financial assistance to injured
workers irrespective of the manner in which the injury was
received. The benefit paid was based on the man's age, size
of family, length of service, and his faithfulness.[80] On

76 ibid., p. 115.
77 National Civic Federation, Conference on Welfare Work, op.
cit., p. 193.
78 Stevens, George A., and Hatch, Leonard W., "Employers' Welfare Institutions", Third Annual Report of the Commissioner
of Labor, New York State Department of Labor, (1904), p. 252.
79 Sickness benefits were more common and will be discussed
in connection with employee benefit associations.
80 Beyer, David S., op. cit., p. 236. In 1909, more than
$7,000 was distributed for this purpose by the American Steel
and Wire Company.

May 1, 1910, the International Harvester Company also began to
compensate injured employees using a plan which closely paralleled
the system used by the United States Steel Corporation.[81] In
the spring of 1910, the National Metal Trades Association inaugurated a mutual insurance scheme by which employees in shops
managed by its members could procure insurance covering sickness
as well as accidents at a cost of $1.00 per month.[82] About
1898, the Brooklyn Rapid Transit Company created a fund of
$10,000 which it used for prizes to be given to men who main-
tained excellent safety records.[83]

Industrial Diseases

　　　Little was known about diseases which were caused and aggra-
vated by industrial working conditions. In 1911, Frederick L.
Hoffman wrote: "The actual and relative extent of industrial
diesases in America cannot be stated with even approximate
accuracy at the present time. Our system of factory inspection
is inadequate and woefully lacking in the required medical
assistants who alone can provide the necessary technical ability
for qualified inquiry into the actual conditions of health and
life in modern industry. The annual reports of our state

81 Clark, Lindley D., "Recent Action Relating to Employers'
　　Liability and Workmen's Compensation", Bulletin No. 90
　　(Washington: Government Printing Office, September, 1910),
　　p. 690.
82 ibid., p. 700
83 Gilman, Nicholas P., A Dividend to Labor, p. 282.

factory inspectors contain very little information."[84] Most
types of occupational diseases were not covered by restrictive
legislation.[85] Where statutory restrictions had been enacted,
as in the case of dust prevention, the mandate was often
ambiguous and in practice more or less ineffective.[86]

Lead poisoning had been pushed into the limelight by 1910
and several paint and mining companies made efforts to combat
it. In a paper presented before the Fourth Annual Convention
of the American Association for Labor Legislation, F. V. Hamar
of the Hamar Lead Works, East St. Louis, explained that the
company stressed prevention (1) through providing ample facilities
for washing and by careful ventilation of the workplace, and
(2) through prompt medical attention.[87] Most industrial firms,
however, ignored the problems created by occupational diseases.

Medical and Hospital Services

One of the first medical departments to be established
in industry was that introduced by the Crane Company in 1866.

---

84 Hoffman, Frederick L., "Industrial Diseases in America",
   American Labor Legislation Review, 1, No. 1, (January, 1911),
   p. 35.
85 First National Conference on Industrial Diseases, Memorial
   on Occupational Diseases, a paper presented to the President
   of the United States on September 29, 1910, p. 126.
86 Hoffman, Frederick L., "Legal Protection from Injurious
   Dusts", American Labor Legislation Review, 1, No. 2,
   (June, 1911), p. 110. Ten states had laws dealing with dust
   control but their enforcement was generally nullified by
   stipulations such as "dusts are to be removed as far as
   practicable".
87 Parkinson, Thomas I., op. cit., pp. 78 and 79.

This company later operated a sanatorium for disabled employees.[88]
A number of firms employed physicians to take care of sick
employees at the company during specified hours and in some
cases to visit such employees at their homes when called. This
arrangement was put into effect at the Swift Company[89] and the
Siegel-Cooper Department Store as early as 1890.[90] At the Bibb
Manufacturing Company of Macon, Georgia such service was provided
to its employees without cost prior to 1900.[91] The W. L. Douglas
Shoe Company, Brockton, Massachusetts arranged for a doctor and
nurse to be available at the factory during the noon hour.[92]
The Strawbridge and Clothier Department Store, Philadelphia
employed a woman physician three days a week and sent employees
in poor health to the seashore at company expense.[93] The
employment of a doctor as a part-time or full-time employee at
the company was uncommon during this period and where this
service was provided the employees frequently helped to finance
it.[94]

---

88 Frankel, Lee K., and Fleischer, Alexander, The Human Factor in
   Industry (New York: The Macmillan Company, 1920), p. 164.
89 ibid., p. 164.
90 Tolman, William H., Industrial Betterment, p. 18. Employees
   helped pay for his services with assessments based on salary
   ranging from ten to forty cents monthly.
91 ibid. The Employee Benefit Association of the Gorham Manufacturing Company employed a physician who visited the company
   daily. Medical services of some sort were also provided by
   the Solvay Process Company, the Brooklyn Bridge Railway
   Company, the Proctor and Gamble Company, and the Pope
   Manufacturing Company.
92 Tolman, William H., Social Engineering, p. 101.
93 Olmstead, Victor H., op. cit., p. 1150.
94 National Association of Employment Managers, First Annual
   Convention, op. cit., p. 14.

Early in our industrial development, it was not uncommon for the wife of the employer to visit sick employees. The initial use of a trained nurse in industry occurred in 1895 when the Vermont Marble Company provided this service to its sick workers and their families. In 1897, the benefit association of a large department store hired a nurse to visit and care for its sick members. The Waltham Watch Company also introduced a nursing service during this period. There is no indication that this practice was widespread.

Physical Examinations

Physical Examinations as a prerequisite to employment were not unknown in this period. The National Cash Register Company inaugurated this practice for new employees in 1901.[95] Edwin L. Shuey, writing in 1900, stated that "quite a number of factories require as a preliminary to employment, an examination by a physician both for factory and office work."[96] This practice evidently made little headway since as late as 1917, W. Irving Clark wrote:[97]

The physical examination of factory employees is

95 Frankel, Lee K., and Fleischer, Alexander, op. cit., p. 164.
96 Shuey, Edwin L., op. cit., p. 47.
97 Clark, Irving W., "Physical Examination and Medical Supervision of Factory Employees", Boston Medical and Surgical
   Journal, 176, No. 7, (February, 1917), pp. 1 and 2. In
   1916, Magnus W. Alexander of the General Electric Company,
   West Lynn, Massachusetts wrote in a personal letter to W.
   Irving Clark that he had just completed a personal survey
   of medical examinations in industrial firms. He reported

a comparatively new undertaking. Previous to
five years ago, except in Chicago, there was,
so far as I know, no physical examination of
employees by any factory in the United States.
About 1910, an anti-tuberculosis society of
Chicago, under the efficient management of Dr.
Sachs, succeeded in interesting a group of
employers in the physical examination of their
employees for tuberculosis. Following this
work, other factories began considering the
advisability of establishing examinations with
the point of view of increasing the efficiency
of their force and assisting in the tuberculosis movement, which at that time was sweep-
ing the country. In 1911, the Norton Company
at Worcester, Massachusetts started examining
its employees.

Hospital Facilities

As early as 1867, the Southern Pacific Railroad Company

rented a residence in Sacramento, California for a temporary

hospital and in 1869 built the first hospital in this country

for the care of employees.[98] Emergency hospitals, staffed by

full-time doctors, were established by the Colorado Fuel and

Iron Company at each of its camps and by the American Steel

and Wire Company.[99] The latter company maintained twenty

well-equipped hospitals. Serious accident cases, however, were

---

that of 300 questionnaires sent to large firms in the United
States, only 35 reported the use of physical examinations for
new employees.
98 Frankel, Lee K., and Fleischer, Alexander, op. cit., p. 164.
This was financed in part by a monthly assessment paid by
employees. Not all railroads provided private hospitals,
but made arrangements instead with independent hospitals
along their lines for admission and treatment of their
employees on liberal terms. In addition, emergency hospitals
were sometimes maintained at terminal points in charge of
company doctors.
99 Beyer, David S., op. cit., p. 234. Among the other companies

sent to public hospitals at company expense.[100] Doctors at
the various camps of the Colorado Fuel and Iron Company gave
monthly lectures on health topics to school children and to
adults in evening courses. A free monthly bulletin, devoted
to sanitation and similar subjects, was circulated without
charge to all employees.[101] The Cleveland Cliffs-Iron Company,
as did other mining companies, maintained hospital and medical
services financed by their employees. The company assumed the
responsibility for making deductions and arranging for the
needed services with local doctors and hospitals.[102] Both H. J.
Heinz Company and the John B. Stetson Company established
hospitals before 1900.[103]

A number of companies paid local hospitals or doctors to
provide their employees with medical services. The Ludlum
Steel and Spring Company, Pompton, New Jersey and the New York
Switch and Crossing Company, Hoboken, New Jersey made annual
payments to the Paterson General Hospital which treated injured
or sick employees free of charge.[104]

which maintained emergency hospital facilities were the
United States Shoe Company, the Iron Clad Manufacturing
Company, the Cleveland Hardware Company, and the Endicott-
Johnson Company.
100 ibid.
101 Tolman, William H., Social Engineering, p. 96.
102 Gilman, Nicholas P., A Dividend to Labor, p. 221.
103 Tolman, William H., Social Engineering, p. 8.
104 ibid., p. 98. Similar contracts were made by the Standard
Bleachery Company and the Ferris Brothers Company.

Conclusion

This chapter has considered the activities of employers
that have to do with the selection and training of workers
and with programs designed to ensure safe working conditions
and to maintain the health of employees.

In this period there was little awareness of the basic
importance of selection in employee-employer relations. The
B. F. Goodrich Company and the Westinghouse Electric and
Manufacturing Company had organized employment departments by
the close of the century, but few companies followed their
example. Toward the end of the period there was some discussion
of the problem as well as of the hiring methods, but the selection
procedures in use were crude in relation to present-day hiring
practices.

Employee training and education received far more attention.
The growing shortage of skilled craftsmen resulting from the
breakdown of the apprenticeship system and the decline in the
immigration of skilled workmen led manufacturing and railroad
companies to establish corporation schools. By 1910, fifteen
manufacturing companies and fourteen railroads had inaugurated
such programs. Moreover, a number of companies were cooperating
with public schools in the conduct of part-time and half-time
industrial education. Some of the corporations established
institutes of their own for the purpose of developing their

employees. The New York City Railway Company introduced a training program for motormen -- the first application of training to a semi-skilled occupation. A few companies became interested in vocational guidance, more of them in providing an opportunity to their employees to take non-industrial courses, and still more of them in supplying information through various types of company publications.

Industrial accidents also received increasing attention but employers generally did not engage in safety work. The United States Steel Corporation carried on intensive work in this area and developed an approach which set a pattern for the safety first movement that developed in subsequent years. Some states passed laws requiring employers to provide safe working conditions, but this legislation apparently was not very effective. Workmen's compensation laws, which spear-headed the drive to reduce industrial accidents in later years, had not been enacted. Employer efforts to deal with industrial accidents were largely centered on the provision of mechanical safeguards and the removal of hazards. Little was known or done about occupational diseases.

A number of companies employed part-time and full time physicians prior to 1900, and some companies established hospitals for their own employees. Other companies worked out arrangements with local hospitals and physicians. Some companies made use of physical examinations, particularly when employees were hired.

CHAPTER VII

ADMINISTRATION OF PERSONNEL ACTIVITIES

In the preceding chapters, we have discussed specific personnel devices and activities introduced by employers during the twenty years beginning in 1890. In most of the companies which experimented with these programs, their administration was decentralized. Many companies assigned one or more of these many activities to an executive, who in turn delegated the work involved to some employee -- a foreman who was about to retire, an older skilled employee, or a company guard. Sometimes, the company hired specialists from the outside -- a physician to direct the medical program, a nurse to give first aid and keep health records, a public school teacher with a knowledge of manual training and some trade skill to administer apprenticeship training and to coordinate job training with class instruction in the schools, a Y. M. C. A. secretary to handle recreation, or a social worker to make family visits and to supervise girls' clubs and related activities.

The number of these functions made effective administration difficult when supervised by busy line executives. Moreover, the interdependence of many of the activities undoubtedly led to duplication and overlapping of efforts. In was to be expected, therefore, that sometime in the development of the personnel movement, companies would place the responsibility for administration in a single executive.

172

The Social Secretary

One of the first attempts to concentrate the administration of a number of personnel activities in a single full-time person was the creation of the position of Social Secretary. The use of a social secretary, who would supervise related personnel activities, was suggested in 1900 by William H. Tolman, who had just returned from Paris where he had been studying social economy.[1] The idea was adopted by the H. J. Heinz Company and the Colorado Fuel and Iron Company in 1901. Other companies which followed the leadership of these companies were the Ludlow Manufacturing Company, Joseph Bancroft and Sons of Wilmington, the Pilgrim Steam Laundry, the Shepard Company of Providence, the Siegel-Cooper Department Store, the R. H. Macy Company, and the Proximity Manufacturing Company of Greensboro.[2]

In 1900, the Cleveland Chamber of Commerce appointed an Industrial Committee to study and improve personnel procedures. After an examination of existing practice, the city hired a social secretary to investigate and improve conditions wherever possible.[3]

The precise functions of the social secretary varied from company to company. William H. Tolman described the activities

---

1 Tolman, William H., Social Engineering (New York: McGraw-Hill Book Company, 1909), p. 49. As far as is known, no attempt to use such secretaries in industry in France had been made.
2 ibid., pp. 55-57.
3 Shuey, Edwin L., Factory People and Their Employers (New York: Lentilhon & Co., 1900), p. 224.

of one of them as follows:[4]

> The Social Secretary at the Pilgrim Steam Laundry
> Company has the supervision and initiative of the
> traveling library of selected books, circulating
> between 200 and 300 volumes a month; weekly talks
> of 15 minutes by the president, welfare manager,
> or invited guests; literature class during winter;
> question box, distribution of pamphlets, verses,
> etc., where most helpful; the free and careful
> use of the medicine chest; prescriptions and
> advice given to workers free; ice water during
> summer months; trips to various points of
> interest on Saturday afternoons; theater parties
> when possible; tickets for special occasions;
> mutual aid society for benefits in case of
> illness or death; Penny Provident for saving
> pennies; bringing odds and ends to give
> others less fortunate.

In some instances, the social secretary served primarily
as a welfare worker. This is revealed by a description of her
duties by the Social Secretary of the Siegel-Cooper Department
Store before the Conference on Welfare Work in 1904;[5]

> I visit their homes very frequently---under all
> circumstances of illness or distress always, and
> get into their home lives. I know the home lives
> of a great many of them. I visit them and help
> them, and it is never mentioned to any one and
> no one knows it except the person or the family
> and myself. I have at my disposal a sum of money
> placed in my hands the first of each month. That
> money is used at my own discretion for the relief
> of the people in the store as I think they need
> it, and no one knows it except myself when any of
> it is used for this purpose.
> I have nothing whatever to do with wages.

The Social Secretary of the Shepard Company functioned
mainly as a "housemother." Before this same Conference, she

---

4 Tolman, William H., Social Engineering, p. 57.
5 National Civic Federation, Proceedings, Conference on Welfare
  Work (New York: Andrew H. Kellogg Company, 1904) p. 109.

reported:[6]

> In our establishment the girls come to me, and
> even the men. There is scarcely a person in the
> house but will at some time come to me for some
> sort of advice or for directions as to where they
> can get this thing or that, and how it can be
> provided. I have often taken the matter under
> investigation and shown them how to do it. It
> is astonishing to see how many women do not know
> how to sew.

The Social Secretary at the Joseph Bancroft & Sons Company
was assigned duties quite similar to those performed by her
counterpart at the Pilgrim Steam Laundry Company. In addition,
however, she acted as the representative of the employees and
brought any grievances to the attention of department heads and
other management representatives.[7]

The Social Secretary at Filene's & Sons, Boston, was
assigned the responsibility for improving the conditions of
the workers, for handling social and welfare duties such as
have been previously described, and for making recommendations
on such crucial matters as wage increases, promotions, and
transfers. She also acted as a representative for employees
where grievances were involved and assisted in the employment
of new workers.[8]

The name, "Social Secretary", was objected to by some of
the companies. It was believed that the term did not reflect
the scope of the work and the responsibilities that were assigned

6 ibid., p. 113.
7 Tolman, William H., Social Engineering, p. 56.
8 National Civic Federation, Conference on Welfare Work, op.
  cit., p. 29.

to this position. At the Conference on Welfare Work of the
National Civic Federation in 1904, it was agreed to substitute
the term, "Welfare Manager."[9] This new name soon came into
vogue and replaced that of social secretary.

The Establishment of Departments to Handle Personnel Functions

In 1901, the Colorado Fuel and Iron Company organized
a sociological department. Dr. R. W. Corwin, chief of the
company's corps of surgeons, was appointed superintendent and
was made responsible for the supervision "of all matters
pertaining to education and sanitary conditions and any other
matters which should assist in bettering the conditions under
which our men live."[10]

Administration of the numerous activities and programs
which the National Cash Register Company maintained for the
benefit of its employees was placed in the hands of its Advance
Department.[11] The direction of the extensive work of this
department was placed in the hands of a welfare director and
three assistants. A summary of its activities included:[12]

> A kindergarten with 100 pupils; a school of
> mechanics, meeting Thursday evening (some 300

9 Tolman, William H., Social Engineering, p. 49.
10 Hanger, G. W. W., "Housing of the Working People in the United
   States", U. S. Department of Commerce and Labor, Bulletin No.
   54, (Washington: Government Printing Office, 1904), p. 1199.
11 Shuey, Edwin L., op. cit., p. 27.
12 Gilman, Nicholas P., A Dividend To Labor, A Study Of Employers'
   Welfare Institutions, (Boston: Houghton, Mifflin and Company,
   1899), p. 231.

men in the company's employ study in various
schools); a small library, which is also a
branch of the Dayton Public Library; an industrial
school for 110 girls on Saturday morning; a
cooking class for about the same number twice
a week; sewing and cooking classes for women;
a millinery school; the boys' gardens; a penny
bank, and a kitchen-garden for children; the
domestic economy department; a dancing school
with three classes; a boy's club; an autoharp
club; a janitors' glee club (twenty-four members);
a band and orchestra; and boys' and girls' gymnasium classes. Most of these activities centre
in the N. C. R. House, which is also a kind of
social settlement on the small scale, with a
deaconess in charge.

The International Harvester Company directed the personnel
activities introuded in its various branch plants from a central
department in Chicago. The Westinghouse Air Brake Company and
the Patton Paint Company also attempted to centralize their
personnel functions.

Administration Through the Y. M. C. A.

Railroad companies and some industrial firms turned over
the organization and administration of personnel activities for
their employees to the Young Men's Christian Association. As
pointed out earlier, the Railroad Branch of this organization at
the close of the period under study maintained 174 clubs or
associations which permitted members to eat, sleep, and enjoy
extensive recreational facilities for an annual fee which
ranged from $3.00 to $5.00 per year.[13]

The Industrial Department of the Y. M. C. A. also conducted

---

13 Tolman, William H., Social Engineering, p. 180.

personnel work in other industries. By 1904, the work of this
branch included the administration of personnel activities at
the Proctor Marble Company, the Lorain Steel Company, and the
Pearl River Lumber Company. The Brooklyn Rapid Transit Railroad
Company also utilized its services on numerous occasions. This
organization placed much emphasis on religious activities. At
the Conference on Welfare Work of the National Civic Federation
in 1904, C. C. Michner, head of the Industrial Department, stated:
"We have been trying to develop shop Bible Classes and on November
1 last we had 175 manufacturing establishments in 115 cities in
North America with an average weekly attendance of 25,000 work-
ingmen at the noon and midnight shop Bible Classes."[14] This
particular aspect of the program never received enthusiastic
endorsement from most employers. It is said to have been a
contributing factor in the failure of the Y. M. C. A. in
industrial personnel work.[15]

Employee Participation in Administration of Personnel Activities

Previous chapters disclosed that employees sometimes

---

14 National Civic Federation, Conference on Welfare Work, op.
cit., p. 79.
15 The Westinghouse Air Brake Company utilized its services for
a short while but proclaimed the venture unsuccessful due to
a lack of industrial understanding on the part of those who
administered the work. The National Cash Register Company
reported a similar failure. The hostile attitude of employers
was evident in the comments and questions which followed Mr.
Michner's speech before the Conference on Welfare Work of the
National Civic Federation.

played a part in the administration of housing, dining, and
recreational activities. A few companies provided for more
extensive participation. Filene's and Sons Company of Boston
accomplished this result through the Filene Cooperative Association which appointed committees to promote greater employee
efficiency and to provide social opportunities for its members.[16]
Employees served on an Arbitration Committee which reviewed
discharges and handled grievances. The Association, through
its officers and committees, worked closely with the company's
Social Secretary.[17]

Several companies, including the Patton Paint Company,
the Pilgrim Steam Laundry, and the S. E. Packard & Sons Company,
organized committees of supervisors for the purpose of improving
working conditions.[18] The Pilgrim Steam Laundry also encouraged
and received recommendations from a committee of employees which
met weekly.[19] The Edison Electric Illuminating Company of New
York provided for employee participation through its Labor
Council. One of the primary functions of this group was to
review suggestions and make recommendations with respect to
the safety, comfort, and convenience of the employees.[20]

16 National Civic Federation, Conference on Welfare Work,
   op. cit., p. 31.
17 Ibid., p. 34.
18 Gilman, Nicholas P., op. cit., p. 292.
19 Tolman, William H., Social Engineering, p. 31.
20 ibid., p. 268.

Conclusion

The need for centralizing the many personnel activities
and functions that were being carried out by progressive companies
became apparent at the turn of the century. A few dozen companies
experimented with social secretaries or created departments
which brought these activities under one head. Some companies,
especially railroad organizations, worked through the Y. M. C. A.
In a few instances, an attempt was made to permit employees to
assist in the administration of the work.

The movement toward centralization, however, did not really
get underway until after the close of World War I.

CHAPTER VIII

AN APPRAISAL

Previous chapters have examined the specific personnel
activities and programs engaged in by employers in the period
under study. This chapter will appraise these innovations.

Any evaluation of these programs should take into consideration the social and moral climate in which the employers thought
and acted. Currently acceptable standards of labor and industrial
relations do not constitute a fair basis for understanding and
evaluating the past. Techniques and actions which were viewed
by contemporaries as courageous forward steps, today appear as
fumbling, unimaginative efforts to deal with the problems of
the time. Evaluation must be tempered by the knowledge that
hindsight gives students in this field a backdrop of achieve-
ments, little dreamed of in this earlier period, against which
to project these initial experiments.

The Nature and Utilization of Personnel Work in this Period

The personnel activities of this period have frequently
been described as "welfare work." Sometimes the name "industrial
betterment" was applied. The term "welfare work" was probably
taken from the German phrase "wohlfahrts einrichtungen" which
was applied to similar activities undertaken by German employers,
Unfortunately, the American translation carried a connotation of
charity or paternalism which apparently was less true of the

German phrase. In any event, the term was subjected to much
criticism and was discontinued after World War I.

The Department of Commerce and Labor summarized the personnel work of this period in 1909. A portion of that summary
follows:[1]

> The various measures for the improvement of the
> condition of workingmen, found in successful opera-
> tion in the establishments visited may be summarized
> as follows:
> 1.   Club organizations in which employees are banded
> together for social, educational, recreative, and
> other purposes incident to such associations.
> 2.   The encouragement of physical culture by means
> of gymnasiums, calisthenics, baseball, bicycle,
> and similar clubs.
> 3.   The improvement of intellectual conditions by
> means of free lectures, libraries, kindergartens,
> and educational classes.
> 4.   The increasing of industrial efficiency through
> industrial schools and manual-training classes.
> 5.   The advancement of spiritual life by means of
> Sunday schools and general religious work.
> 6.   The cultivation of musical taste and ability by
> means of concerts and musical entertainments for
> employees, and the encouragement of musical clubs
> and organizations among them.
> 7.   The promotion of improved social conditions
> by means of social gatherings, summer outings,
> meeting places, and game rooms for employees,
> banquets, dances, etc.
> 8.   The sharing of profits with employees.
> 9.   The promotion of employees' personal interest
> in the successful conduct of the business by
> encouraging and assisting them to purchase shares
> in it, thus, in effect, taking them into partner-
> ship.
> 10. The improvement of domestic conditions by
> means of improved dwellings, instruction in sewing,
> cooking, and housekeeping, and in landscape and
> kitchen gardening and the exterior and interior
> decoration of homes.

---

1 Olmstead, Victor H., "The Betterment of Industrial Conditions",
U. S. Department of Commerce and Labor, Bulletin No. 31, (Washington: Government Printing Office, 1900), p. 117-8.

11. The care for employees' health and comfort by
means of bathing facilities, dining and lunch
rooms, the furnishing of hot lunches to female
employees, and by improved sanitary construction
and appliances.
12. The care of sick and disabled employees and
their families by means of free insurance, free
medical attendance or hospital facilities, and
by the encouragement of beneficial organizations.
13. The cultivation of thrift through savings
bank facilities, building associations, or
provident organizations, and by the giving of
prizes for valuable suggestions of employees
and rewards for faithful service or the manifestation of zeal and interest in their employment.
14. The rendering of financial aid to employees in cases of hardship or distress.
15 The manifestation of interest in the personal
affairs of individual employees, the cultivation
of cordial and even confidential relations with
them, and the promotion of their welfare in all
possible ways.

The personnel work of this period was arbitrarily classified

into 22 categories, including external plant improvements, in-

ternal plant improvements, rest rooms and rest periods, mis-

cellaneous improvements in working conditions, centralized

administration of personnel work, selection and promotion,

training (all types), publications, safety and medical, indoor

recreation, outdoor recreation, miscellaneous services (including

vacations), dining facilities, hours, incentive wage payment

plans, profit sharing, stock purchase plans and cooperative

purchasing, pensions, insurance, building and loan and savings

plans, suggestion systems, and housing and communal betterment.

The above categories of personnel activities sound very

impressive. It must be remembered, however, that their application

in industry was greatly restricted and that the actual conduct
of many of them was so elementary that the appellation used to
describe them was hardly justified.

As we have seen, the literature of this period disclosed
much interest in various aspects of personnel work. One must
conclude, however, that this interest did not give rise to a
widespread introduction of personnel programs and activities.
In fact, only a minority of companies engaged in this work.

This survey of betterment or welfare programs in industry
uncovered only 302 companies that had undertaken such work
during this twenty-year period. When this number is compared
to a total of more than 268,000 manufacturing firms in existence
in 1910, the limited scope of the personnel function is eminently
clear. Moreover, of these 300-odd firms, some 208 firms, about
69 per cent, had introduced only one personnel activity. Only
20 firms, fewer than 7 per cent, had introduced five or more
specific activities.[2] The National Cash Register Company was
the outstanding participant in these activities. Near the top
of the list were the Natural Food Company, the H. J. Heinz

---

2   These companies were the Acme Lead and Color Works; the
    Colorado Fuel and Iron Company; Filene's and Sons; the Gorham
    Manufacturing Company; the H. J. Heinz Company; the Inter-
    national Harvester Company; the Ludlow Manufacturing Company;
    the National Cash Register Company; the Natural Food Company;
    the N. O. Nelson Company; the Peacedale Manufacturing Company;
    the Plymouth Cordage Company; the Proctor and Gamble Company;
    the Sherwin-Williams Paint Company; the Siegel-Cooper Depart-
    ment Store; the Solvay Process Company; the John B. Stetson
    Company; the Strawbridge and Clothier Department Store; the
    Westinghouse Electric and Manufacturing Company, and the J.
    H. Williams Company.

Company, the Plymouth Cordage Company, the John B. Stetson
Company, the Ludlow Manufacturing Company, the Solvay Process
Company, and the Westinghouse Electric and Manufacturing
Company.

A further indication of the limited scope of personnel
activity was reported by William H. Tolman in 1909:[3]

> The Industrial Committee of the Cleveland
> Chamber of Commerce, formed in 1900, reported
> shortly after its inception on the extent of
> "industrial betterment" carried on by its
> members. Of the two thousand members of the
> Chamber, four hundred and fifty are employers
> of labor. The report of the study made showed
> that twenty-five of these firms were engaged
> in some form of industrial betterment. A
> subsequent study made in 1908 showed that
> approximately two hundred employers were
> interested in some form of it.

A study of welfare work made in 1903 by the New York State
Department of Labor showed that some betterment work was being
carried on by 110 establishments.[4] The findings of these studies
were verified by a comprehensive study of welfare work undertaken
by the Bureau of Labor Statistics over a period of twelve months
in 1916 and 1917.[5] The Bureau survey reported that 431 establishments had undertaken one or more welfare activities. The number

---

3 Tolman, William H., _Social Engineering_ (New York: McGraw-
Hill Book Co., 1909), p. 46.
4 Stevens, George A., and Hatch, Leonard W., "Employers'
Welfare Institutions", _Third Annual Report of the Commissioner
of Labor_, New York State Department of Labor, (1904), p. 227.
5 Reported in United States Department of Labor, Bureau of Labor
Statistics, "Welfare Work for Employees in Industrial Establishments in the United States", Vol. 250 (Washington: Government
Printing Office, February, 1919), pp. 7-139. The nature of the
study which covered 31 states was described as follows: "...the

of establishments engaged in such activities is specified by industries in Table I. Speaking of the period prior to 1910, the author of this report wrote: "It is safe to say that, with the exception of a comparatively few of these establishments, the major part of the progress along these lines would extend over only the last 10 or 12 years."[6] The evidence is overwhelming that betterment or personnel work had not yet moved any great distance from the novelty or experimental stage by 1910.

Table I

Welfare Work in Industrial Establishments[1]

Industry	Number of Companies
Textiles	60
Foundries and Machine Shops	49
Stores	47
Iron and Steel	40
Electric Railroads	17
Food Products	15
Telephone and Telegraph	15
Clothing and Furnishings	13
Coal Mining	12
Other Mining	12
Gas and Electric Power	10
Printing and Publishing	10
Steam Railroads	10

investigation was concerned with so-called welfare work as entirely separate and distinct from other phases of employment. Wages might be low, hours long, working conditions bad, and tenure of employment insecure, but if the establishment had, before correcting these obvious evils, installed a good lunch room, wash room, or other welfare feature, it was visited and scheduled for that alone. However, as a general rule, establishments doing the most along welfare lines have superior conditions in the other directions mentioned."
6 ibid., p. 119.

Table I (continued)

Industry	Number of Companies
Automobiles	9
Offices	9
Rubber and Composition Goods	9
Fine Machines and Instruments	8
Chemical and Allied Products	7
Paper and Paper Goods	7
Boots and Shoes	5
Electrical Supplies	5
Explosives	5
Miscellaneous Industries (fewer than 5 companies)	57
TOTAL	431

1 United States Department of Labor, Bureau of Labor Statistics, op. cit., p. 7.

Forces and Conditions Influencing the Growth of Personnel Work

What were the forces and conditions that prompted employers to re-examine their relationships with their employees and to embark on various personnel programs? One of the important factors which was altering this relationship was the growth in the size of the individual firm. It is difficult to evaluate the impact of this factor on employer thinking, but the loss of a personal relationship between employer and employee was recognized at least as early as 1899 when Nicholas P. Gilman wrote:[7]

> In older times, when the master worked side by side with his men, in the field or the small shop, or was at least familiarly known to them,

7 Gilman, Nicholas P., A Dividend to Labor, A Study of Employers' Welfare Institutions (Boston: Houghton, Mifflin and Company, 1899), p. 18.

the acquaintanceship had its natural result,
in most cases, in a general sympathy and
friendliness which greatly facilitated produ-
tion. The progress of invention, the immense
development of industrial organization and the
wide prevalence of corporate methods have
rendered difficult, if not impossible, the old
friendliness based on personal knowledge. But
a substitute is not impossible, which shall
manifest the interest of the employer in those
who work for him.

It was the belief of the more progressive employers that

some substitute would have to be found to restore the mutual

understanding that tended to prevail in smaller organizations.

In 1909, William H. Tolman wrote: "As is clearly recognized,

the personal touch between employer and employee has been

largely lost, and it is not desirable, even if it were possible,

to return to the earlier days but for the successful conduct

of the business man today, a point of contact must be established

in some way."[8]

Some industrial leaders tried to get closer to their

employees through various informal procedures. An executive of

the Sherwin-Williams Paint Company explained the practice

followed by his company at the Conference on Welfare Work of

the National Civic Federation:[9]

We do everything we can to get closer to our
men; and among other things, we have our
evenings together. The President, Vice-
president, and all the other members of the

---

8 Tolman, William H., Social Engineering, p. 82.
9 National Civic Federation, Proceedings, Conference on Welfare
  Work (New York: Andrew H. Kellogg Co., 1904), p. 131.

company meet with our employees about once a
week, and they have their papers -- these
papers are read by the different employees,
some by the foremen, some by the workmen. We
have evenings spent that way.

Others believed that they could overcome the effects of
large scale production through a spirit of friendliness and a
guarantee that employees were always welcome to voice their
sentiments and complaints to top management. As typical of
this approach, one employer was quoted as saying:[10]

I cannot know all my men now as I did formerly,
but I still know a large number of them especially
those that have been with me for a long period....
I try to go through the shops as often as I can
and shake hands with the men and talk with them
of their work....My men feel that they can see me
at any and all times, I do not shut myself up
in a private office....I see and listen to all.

To the writer it would seem that many of the personnel
programs particularly those providing recreation, general education, improvement of working conditions, sharing of profits,
better housing, dining facilities, care of sick and disabled,
financial aid at times of distress, and home visits, consciously
or unconsciously, were in part attempts to bridge the wide gap
that had developed between employers and employees.

Another factor was the growing criticism of social workers
and students of labor and economics of the factory system and
its impact upon the industrial worker. Undoubtedly this factor
influenced the introduction of employers' programs which im-

10 Foote, Mark, "How the Conquerors of Business Win", System, VIII,
No. 2, (August, 1905), p. 108.

proved working conditions, reduced hours of work, and sought to insure the physical well-being and health of employees. Other programs may well have been introduced partially for this reason. Of interest on this point are the comments of the President of the J. H. Williams Company:[11]

> We are sensible of the responsibilities of employers to employees, and have therefore observed some of the conditions of health, safety and comfort, and our aim has been with our employees to establish good-will, good fellowship and friendly spirit; to lighten their labors and show interest in their welfare; to promote interest and cheerfulness by fair treatment; never to interfere with the freedom of individual conduct; never to allow a faithful employee to be discharged; to avoid paternalism or giving with condescension; and above all to express our appreciation through high wages.

A third factor was the growing industrial unrest which accompanied the long period of falling prices and unemployment that followed the Civil War. This unrest reflected itself in national strikes involving violence and bloodshed during the late eighties and early nineties and in the rapid growth in membership and power of labor organizations during the "honeymoon period", 1898 to 1904. In 1899, Nicholas P. Gilman wrote: "The actual condition of the modern industrial world is one of profound discontent on the part of the great body of men and women who support themselves by hand labor...(It) is the most pronounced of existing discontents, and it forces itself upon

11 Tolman, William H., Social Engineering, p. 360.

public attention with increasing vigor."[12] On this point,
William H. Tolman stated:[13]

> A decade ago when there was a decided impulse
> towards some form of improvement, it was under-
> taken not through altruism but through necessity.
> The awakened intelligence of workmen began to
> voice itself in expressions that something more
> than wages was due them. Hitherto they had
> accepted their surroundings without demur. To
> allay this feeling of smothered discontent, the
> industrialist was forced into attempts at better-
> ment; he felt this step was necessary to hold
> his labor.

Industrial unrest undoubtedly convinced some employers that
something constructive should be done to deal with the situation
and to remove as far as possible the causes of dissatisfaction
and discontent. Profit sharing was one of the specific devices
introduced by some employers to assure greater social justice.
Henry R. Towne, as early as 1886, in a paper before the American
Society of Mechanical Engineers, urged the development of wage
systems to share the profits of business with employees on the
basis of their productive efficiency. This factor probably
helped to inspire the introduction of many of the "welfare"
programs.

A fourth factor that led to the adoption of personnel
activities was location and the absence of essential community
facilities. Companies establishing plants and mines in isolated

---

12 Gilman, Nicholas P., Profit Sharing Between Employer and
   Employee (Boston: Houghton, Mifflin and Company, 1889), p. 1.
13 Tolman, William H., Social Engineering, p. 365.

areas found it necessary to provide extensive welfare programs
and facilities and sometimes to build a new community.

A fifth factor which may have exerted an influence on
employers was a greater social consciousness toward needy and
less privileged individuals. This was evidenced, in part, by
the important welfare work being done by voluntary charities
and by individual gifts and bequests for philanthropic purposes.[14]
Public welfare work, too, had already assumed an important place
in the care of these persons.[15] No evidence, however, has been
found to indicate that this had a specific influence on the
personnel work of the period.

Employer Motivation and Personnel Work

Employers attributed their increased interest in employee
welfare to many things. Some testified that this interest was
primarily due to an awakened sense of obligation to their
employees. Their objectives, it was claimed, were altruistic
or philanthropic. The President of the W. D. Forbes Company
wrote: "The things that are done by our company are without
pressure of any kind from any source. They are simply a free

---

14 In the eleven-year period from 1893 to 1904, the individual
   gifts and bequests from individuals were estimated at more
   than 610 million dollars. (Henderson, Charles R., Modern
   Methods of Charity [New York: The Macmillan Company, 1904],
   p. 413.)
15 In 1902, for example, more than 300,000 persons were supported
   wholly or in part by charity in Massachusetts. The estimated
   cost for this work was more than 5 million dollars. (ibid.)

will offering to the good and welfare of its employees, given
in recognition of the moral obligation devolving upon employers
to consider the reasonable interests and desires of the workmen,
so far as the practical rules of business and the efficient
operation of industry permits this to be done."[16]

Many employers freely acknowledged that they introduced
such programs because it paid them to do so. In 1909, the superintendent of the Waltham Watch Company wrote:[17]

> We do not believe in nor practice "Paternalism."
> Nevertheless, it is our policy and constant aim
> to create pleasant surroundings for our people,
> for aside from any humanitarian sentiment, which
> we do not at all disclaim, we are confident that
> the moral effect of the attractive conditions which
> we aim to establish is such as to constitute a
> wise business policy....A good many centuries ago
> the statement was made that "Godliness is profitable,"
> and while the original assertion had an individual
> application, it may be no violence to the original
> maxim to assert its truth as applied to business,
> at least, to the extent of asserting that it "pays
> to be considerate."

One of the most frequently cited advantages of personnel
work was that it enabled the firm to attract and retain desirable
employees. The following comment of one executive is typical:
"We might add, in summing up in a general way, that one marked
result of incorporating into our business some of these methods,
has been the fact that we are enabled to-day to secure a better
class of help, more intelligent, and doing better work than it
was possible to secure before."[18] An official of another

16 Tolman, William H., Social Engineering, p. 360.
17 ibid., p. 362.
18 Shuey, Edwin L., Factory People and Their Employers (New

company stated:[19]

> We are not forced to do these things, but we like
> to do them, and the men appreciate what is being
> done in this direction. We pay them well and
> give them additional things. We want to make the
> conditions so pleasant that a machinist would
> rather work for us than anywhere else. We have
> not hired a new machinist in three years, which
> fact proves that the men are satisfied with their
> employment here, and also that our policy attracts
> to us the best class of mechanics, for we have not
> had occasion in that time to discharge any of them
> for incompetency nor other reason.

Discussing the reasons for his company's extensive participation

in betterment work, S. H. Patterson of the National Cash Register

Company wrote:[20]

> What many of my business associates have character-
> ized as sentimental -- namely, baths in the factory,
> prizes for suggestions, landscape gardening, pleas-
> ant Sunday afternoons, lunches for the girls in the
> office, boys' gardens, and our various clubs -- cost
> us about $30,000, or three per cent of our annual
> pay roll, $1,000,000.
> We buy physical and mental labor. If it pays to
> take care of a good animal that only returns
> physical work, how much more important is it for
> the employer to take care of the employee return-
> ing both physical and mental labor.
> We believe that people are a part of all they
> have met; that is, all they have seen and all they
> have heard is absorbed by them, and it therefore
> pays to have good influences and surroundings for
> them. We have tried both plans, and believe that
> the three per cent of our annual pay roll which
> we spend on movements for industrial betterment
> yields us approximately between five and ten per
> cent profit in actual dollars and cents. The
> morale, the example and daily lives of our em-
> ployees, are influences that refuse to yield to
> statistics.

York: Lentilhon & Co., 1900), p. 200.
19 Stevens, George A., and Hatch, Leonard W., op. cit., p. 310.
20 Tolman, William H., Industrial Betterment (New York: The
   Social Service Press, 1900), p. 81.

Similar testimony reveals that employers in this period believed that personnel work paid for itself. Few, if any, however, substantiated this conviction with financial data. In its 1917 study of welfare programs, the Bureau of Labor Statistics stated that "it is surprising to find that few firms have definite knowledge of what the work is costing them."[21]

Certain personnel functions were undoubtedly introduced to help management meet its day-to-day problems. For example, employee training was necessitated by a rising demand for skilled labor at a time when the old apprenticeship system was breaking up and the immigration of skilled craftsmen was falling away sharply. Employment departments were introduced to uncover through scouting and other devices the much needed skilled labor. Pension plans and other welfare activities were, in part, inaugurated to persuade workers to stay with the company.

Finally, personnel work for some employers was probably a form of insurance against unions. No statistical data are available to support this observation. Moreover, few employers were willing to be as frank as the President of the J. H. Williams Company when he said:[22]

> No labor union exists among our employees. Under present circumstances we do not believe its establishment in our works would be of mutual advantage, although we are not opposed to labor organizations in general....Endeavoring to keep somewhat in personal touch with our employees,

21 United States Department of Labor, Bureau of Labor Statistics, op. cit., p. 118.
22 Stevens, George A., and Hatch, Leonard W., op. cit., p. 266.

and not overlooking the ethical side of our relations, we have enjoyed, for the twenty years
since our business started, satisfactory cooperation.

Basic Shortcomings of the Welfare Movement

The fact that much of what was done during this twenty-
year period has received wide acceptance in industry today
demonstrates the real worth of these early programs. Employers'
efforts to improve working conditions and to provide for the
workers' general welfare and safety deserve the highest commen-
dation. It must be remembered that few legal compulsions prevailed during this period and that only a handful of employers
had attempted to improve general working conditions before 1890.
Most employers were antagonistic to unions and wholly indifferent
to the welfare of their employees. Many of the evils of the
factory system had not been corrected and a large body of employers were in opposition to any improvements. The Commission on
Industrial Relations stated:[23]

> ...evidence has been presented covering the long
> fights to secure legislation to remove the evils
> of company stores, payment in scrip, prison
> labor, arbitrary deductions from wages, "sweat-
> ing," tenement houses, and a number of other
> matters upon which adequate legislation has not
> yet been secured....Evidence has further been
> presented to show that such a condition has not
> been the result entirely of the complacency or
> slothfulness of legislators, but that powerful
> influences have been at work to prevent such
> remedial legislation. The most convincing evi-
> dence presented upon this phase of the question

---

23 Commission on Industrial Relations, United States Senate, Final
Report (Washington: Barnard and Miller Print, 1915), p. 42.

> is the record of the National Association of
> Manufacturers and its allied organizations....
> It is necessary here to call attention only to
> the fact that the efforts of such associations
> in preventing the enactment of practically all
> legislation intended to improve the condition
> or advance the interests of workers were not
> confined to Congress, but were even more effec-
> tive in the State legislatures.

Hours of work were long and arduous and wages, particularly for the unskilled, were kept at very low levels. The average annual wage never exceeded $630 in this period, but the Commission on Industrial Relations, after exhaustive studies, determined that an annual income of $700 was necessary for a family of five to live "with anything approaching decency."[24] The conclusion reached by this investigating body with respect to the basic manufacturing industries and coal mining was that "between one-half and two-thirds of these families were living below the standards of decent subsistence, while about one-third were living in a state which can be described as abject poverty."[25]

Moreover, most workers were denied the opportunity to improve their economic and social status through collective bargaining. Because of the impressive growth of the American Federation of Labor from 1898 to 1904, powerful opposition to organized labor developed. By means of employer associations, resort to the use of injunctions in labor disputes, and efforts to apply

---

24 ibid., p. 10.
25 ibid. The investigation covered 619,595 employees in basic manufacturing industries and in coal mining. It should be pointed out that these industries employed large numbers of unskilled immigrant laborers.

the Sherman Act to labor organizations, employers were able to
hold the growth of the movement in check. The prevailing
attitude of employers was set forth by the Commission on Industrial Relations:[26]

> It is very significant that out of 230 represent-
> atives of the interest of employers, chosen largely
> on the recommendations of their own organizations,
> less than half a dozen have denied the propriety
> of collective action on the part of employees. A
> considerable number of these witnesses have, how-
> ever, testified that they denied in practice what
> they admitted to be right in theory. A majority
> of such witnesses were employers who in the oper-
> ation of their business maintained what they, in
> accordance with the common terminology, called
> the "open shop." The theory of the "open shop,"
> according to these witnesses, is that workers
> are employed without any reference to their member-
> ship or nonmembership in trade unions; while, as
> a matter of fact, it was found upon investigation
> that these employers did not, as a rule, willingly
> or knowingly employ union men.

There was evidence, too, that the legal system was weighted
heavily against the worker. The law was written and interpreted
to protect property rights and, in cases where these rights
clashed with human rights, the former usually took precedence.
The Industrial Relations Commission reported:[27]

> No testimony presented to the Commission has
> left a deeper impression than the evidence that
> there exists among the workers an almost uni-
> versal conviction that they, both as individuals
> and as a class, are denied justice in the enact-
> ment, adjudication, and administration of the
> law, that the very instruments of democracy are
> often used to suppress them and to place obsta-
> cles in the way of their movement towards

---

26 ibid., p. 85.
27 ibid., p. 38.

economic, industrial, and political freedom and
justice.

In a climate such as prevailed in this period, the thesis
that employers have a responsibility for the health, safety, and
well-being of their employees and that productivity and employee
goodwill could be increased by shorter hours, better ventilation,
recreation, profit sharing, wholesome food, and other activities
was a revolutionary idea. Despite the basic worth of these programs, however, they often failed, and despite apparent success
in some firms, the basic objectives were not always attained.
It is pertinent, therefore, to consider the basic limitations
of this movement.

The Absence of a Realistic Philosophy of Human Relations - One
of the shortcomings of the movement was the failure of the employer to convince his workers that he honestly had their best
interests at heart. Employees showed a natural reluctance to
accept a welfare program as a genuine expression of good faith
when the employer simultaneously engaged in other tactics which
seriously abridged basic employee rights or disregarded essential
needs and goals. For example, Andrew Carnegie established a
free library and an elaborate clubhouse for his workers, but
his steel mills operated on a 12-hour day in the face of a bitter
struggle on the part of organized labor to win an 8-hour day.
Many of the railroad companies which were mostly actively engaged
in betterment work maintained a private police force and arsenals

of arms and ammunition. This private army, augmented by re-
cruits from detective and employment agencies, was guilty of
serious encroachments on the rights of their employees and labor
organizers.[28] Moreover, some of the railroad benefit programs
had undesirable features which minimized their acceptability to
employees. Most of the costs of such plans were paid by the
employees, the company paying only the cost of administration.
In addition, the programs served to relieve the companies from
liability for accidents since employees were required to sign
a statement releasing the company from this obligation. Membership was often compulsory, but employees did not share in
its administration, and if the employee left the company for any
cause, he usually forfeited his contribution.[29]

The Pullman Company also operated under conflicting policies.
Although the company provided modern houses for its employees,
it denied its employees the right to affiliate with labor unions.
It achieved this goal by means of an effective system of espionage
and the discharge of employees known to be members of labor unions.[30]
In 1894, when wages were cut 22 per cent and hours of work were
reduced while rents on company-owned houses remained the same,
the employees went out on strike. The company insisted that its
investment in housing was a separate outlay upon which it was
entitled to earn four per cent. As a result of the bitter strike

---

28 ibid., p. 111.
29 ibid.
30 ibid., p. 110.

that ensued, the company disposed of its houses.[31] The Colorado
Fuel and Iron Company, which engaged extensively in betterment
work, failed to win employee goodwill as is evidenced by the
fact that martial law was invoked ten times between 1894 and
1914.[32] During these periods, strikers were imprisoned by military courts, thousands were held in "bull pens," and many were
forcibly deported from the state. Even the National Cash Register
Company, which was the undisputed leader in betterment activities,
had a 7-week strike beginning in May, 1901.[33]

The above examples indicate that many employees were not
very sympathetic to welfare programs as conducted by employers
during this period. Anti-labor sentiment on the part of employers and a disregard of essential goals of workers gave rise
to a natural suspicion and even hostility toward betterment programs. Employers were aware of this resentment. John F. P.
Lawton, of the Gorham Manufacturing Company, explained the resistance his company encountered in constructing a recreation hall:
"When we got pretty well along with the building, I noticed that
the men took very little interest in it. I asked a number of
them about it, and found that they were a little suspicious. We
couldn't seem to convince them that the company did not have some

---

31 Frankel, Lee K., and Fleischer, Alexander, The Human Factor
   in Industry (New York: The Macmillan Company, 1920), p. 269.
32 Commission on Industrial Relations, United States Senate,
   op. cit., p. 73.
33 Tolman, William H., Social Engineering, p. 365.

ulterior motive."[34] C. C. Michner, Secretary of the Industrial
Department of the Y. M. C. A., stated:[35]

> I have been studying this problem for a number of
> years, and in places where this work has been done
> by the company I have yet to find one instance
> where the men themselves are satisfied with what
> the company is doing, and in most places, in
> confidence, the management have told me, in their
> private offices, that it was not working the way
> they had hoped.

Similar statements were made by other employer representatives,
including those of the Solvay Process Company, the National
Battery Company, the Sidney Shepard Company, and the Siegel-
Cooper Department Store.

As a result of this suspicion and resentment of employees,
some employers changed their attitude toward welfare and betterment programs. Particularly interesting is the reaction of one
industrialist:[36]

> We have considerably curtailed our work along the
> lines of industrial betterment, and while we used
> to do considerable of it at one time, we are not
> quite as enthusiastic over it now....Whether it
> was that our people were a class of foreigners who
> did not seem to appreciate the work we attempted
> to do, or whether their appreciation was misunder-
> stood by us, I do not know. I feel perfectly con-
> vinced in my own mind...that it was a mistake to
> continue it; in fact, a mistake to have started
> it....In other words, we shall buy our labor as
> we buy our material, and we are thoroughly con-
> vinced in our own minds that those who sell us
> their labor will give us as little as they possi-
> bly can for what they sell us without regard to

34 National Civic Federation, Conference on Welfare Work, op.
   cit., p. 95.
35 Ibid.
36 Tolman, William H., Social Engineering, p. 356.

whether or not we attempt to go more than our
half of the way on some of these things outside
of those which money can buy.

Welfare Work was Company Initiated and Administered - The failure of betterment work to achieve greater acceptability in this
period must in part be attributed to the fundamental lack of
democracy in its conception, installation, and administration.
Action was generally taken by the employer based on his ideas
of what was best for his employees. For example, dining facilities were installed because the employer felt his employees
were not getting enough wholesome food. Sanitary toilet and
bathing facilities often owed their origin to the employers'
knowledge that these were not available in the workers' homes.
The employer decided that a clubhouse or athletic field should
be established because frequently recreational activities were
not otherwise available or the alternative possibilities did
not meet with his approval. The underlying philosophy appears
to have been one of paternalism. Only rarely were employees
consulted as to the desirability of particular activities or
given an opportunity to share in their administration. This
policy was followed even when employees helped to pay for such
programs.

Given such a philosophy, it is not surprising that employers concentrated so much of their effort on improving the social
and economic welfare of the employees. The unilateral approach

to such work made it seem arbitrary even though the employer's intention was otherwise. It was particularly distasteful when the program was introduced in a condescending manner or administered in a lady bountiful spirit. Resentment of employees toward such work was both natural and understandable.

The most outstanding examples of employer paternalism were found where complete towns had been built around the plant. Textile communities in the South and mining and lumbering towns in the North were outstanding examples of this condition. In these cases, the entire community was frequently dominated by the town's sole employer and benefactor. He not only owned the land on which the town was built, but also exercised control over the community's social and economic life, including the local government, schools, and churches. Of interest are the findings of the Commission on Industrial Relations:[37]

> Under certain conditions where his (employee) individual or corporate employer owns or controls the community in which he lives, the education of his children, the character and prices of his food, clothing, and house, his own actions, speech and opinions, and in some cases even his religion, are controlled and determined, in so far as the interests of the employer make it desirable for him to exercise such control. Such conditions are established and maintained not only through the dictations of all working conditions by the employer, but by his usurpation or control of the functions and machinery of political government in such communities.

Fortunately, these conditions were not typical.

---

[37] Commission on Industrial Relations, United States Senate, op. cit., p. 1.

That paternalism was not in tune with American life is shown by the following examples. In one instance, the workers refused to use a beautiful $40,000 memorial library built by the employer; instead, they collected $8,000 and constructed their own unpretentious building. Evidently, they preferred a less magnificent structure which they themselves could administer and control.[38] Another example involved the Pocasset Worsted Company near Providence, Rhode Island. This company built a $20,000 clubhouse for its employees in 1907. At first membership was free, but later it was raised to $2.00 a year in order to make the employees feel that they were not accepting charity. The memberhsip dwindled from 200 to 60 and eventually, the experiment was discontinued.[39] Undoubtedly Samuel Gompers interpreted the attitude of many American workmen when he pointed out that "this relationship has enveloped the movement (welfare work) with an atmosphere of charity and patronage that is most repugnant to virile, self-reliant workers."[40] The observation of Charles W. Hubbard, Treasurer of the Ludlow Manufacturing Company, is also pertinent:[41]

We often read glowing accounts of social better-

---

38 National Civic Federation, Conference on Welfare Work, op. cit., p. 91.
39 Frankel, Lee K., and Fleischer, Alexander, op. cit., p. 246.
40 Boettiger, Louis A., Employee Welfare Work (New York: The Ronald Press Company, 1923), p. 15.
41 Letter to the Department of Commerce and Labor, quoted in Hanger, G. W. W., "Housing of the Working People in the United States," U. S. Department of Commerce and Labor, Bulletin No.54 (Washington: Government Printing Office, 1904), p. 1213.

ment carried on by such and such a concern; shortly afterwards of the establishment being the
center of a disastrous strike; later, possibly
that the whole attempt at social betterment has
been given up as a failure. Then it is safe to
say that it was not conceived in the right spirit;
that it was either dictated by self-interest or
executed in a spirit of condescending patronage.

It should be pointed out that not all of the programs
introduced by employers during this period fall into the category
of welfare activities. In this group are personnel functions,
such as apprenticeship training, safety programs, better working
conditions, shorter hours, profit sharing, medical work, selection, promotion plans, and stock purchase plans. These plans,
introduced to help solve current management problems, to increase productivity, or lower costs, have been carried on right
up to the present time. Even the so-called welfare activities
are now conducted under the heading of "employee services."
These services are frequently jointly administered. An increasing number of them are becoming subjects included in contract negotiations.

Summary and Conclusions

The twenty-year interval selected for study may be regarded as the formative period of personnel administration.
While some of the activities were first introduced prior to
1890, they were, on the whole, limited to a few companies.
Many of the 22 categories of welfare or betterment work were
initiated in this period and experimentation with them in these

years led employers to appraise their worth. As a result, some
of them were discontinued; others were modified to meet modern
industrial conditions.

Among the factors and conditions that prompted employers
to introduce such activities were (1) the growth in the size of
establishments and companies, the resulting loss of personal
contact, and the lack of mutual understanding that devloped
between workers and management, (2) the growing criticism of
the impact of the factory system upon the well-being of industrial workers, (3) the increasing industrial unrest which
accompanied the period of falling prices and unemployment
after the Civil War, (4) the many strikes, often of a violent
nature, that were conducted during this period, particularly
after the turn of the century, and (5) the absence of community
facilities for citizens in many of the developing geographic
areas of the country.

Two other factors may also have influenced the rise of
personnel administration. As pointed out earlier, there was
an increasing sense of responsibility toward less fortunate
individuals as was demonstrated by the large sums of money set
aside for philanthropic purposes, and by the rise of public
social agencies. The second factor that may have affected the
character of this movement was the growing importance of women
in American life. This is evidenced by the increasing employment of women workers in industry and more particularly by the

utilization of nurses and social secretaries to assist in carrying out betterment programs.

The motives which led to the introduction of these programs and activities were varied, including (1) a growing sense of social responsibility on the part of employers and a genuine concern about the welfare of their employees, (2) a belief that welfare and betterment work would pay for itself in greater productivity, improved products, better morale, a higher grade of employees, lower labor turnover, and therefore, lower costs, (3) the pressure to solve day-to-day problems, such as the shortage of skilled labor, mounting accident rates, and labor turnover, and (4) the desire to keep labor organizations out of the company.

Notwithstanding the forces at work, employers did not hasten to introduce these personnel practices. Only 300-odd companies had initiated work of this nature and only seven per cent of them had five or more activities.

The movement was not based on realistic philosophy of human relations. Generally speaking, the programs were company initiated and administered. The workers resented the paternalistic spirit in which much of this work was undertaken. They wanted a voice in determining their terms of employment and the activities that influenced the conditions under which they made a living. They were unwilling to accept largess for independence.

Some employers introduced employee services and activities of
a social and recreational nature at the expense of higher wages,
shorter hours, and other more important needs and goals of
workers. Many employers denied their employees the right to
organize and bargain collectively. The co-existence of progressive and unenlightened policies and practices led employees
to become suspicious of employer motives and to take a hostile
attitude toward these activities introduced by management.

Nothwithstanding the shortcomings of this developing movement, much of this work filled a basic need and called attention
to conditions in our industrial life that needed to be corrected.
Management became aware of the importance of attitudes in developing constructive employer-employee relations. It also
began to analyze problems of human relationships in the organization and sought to work out systematic procedures for dealing with them. Most of the activities developed in this period
have been refined and incorporated in modern programs of industrial relations, either by management unilaterally or through
the medium of collective bargaining.

BIBLIOGRAPHY

Adams, Thomas S., and Sumner, Helen L., Labor Problems
      (New York: The Macmillan Company, 1905), 579 pp.

Alexander, Magnus W., "The Apprenticeship System of the
      General Electric Company at West Lynn, Massachusetts,"
      The Annals, Vol. 33, No. 1, (January, 1909), pp. 141-150.

American Association for Labor Legislation, "Review of Labor
      Legislation of 1911," American Labor Legislation Review,
      Vol. I, No. 3, (October, 1911), 162 pp.

Beyer, David S., "Safety Provisions in the United States Steel
      Corporation," The Survey, XXIV, (September, 1910), pp.
      205-236.

Boettiger, Louis A., Employee Welfare Work (New York: The
      Ronald Press Company, 1923), 301 pp.

Bowman, Mary Jean and Bach, George L., Economic Analysis and
      Public Policy (New York: Prentice-Hall, Inc., 1949), 931
      pp.

Clark, Lindley D., "Recent Action Relating to Employers' Liability
      and Workmen's Compensation," Bulletin No. 90 (Washington:
      Government Printing Office, September, 1910), p. 690.

Clark, W. Irving, "Physical Examination and Medical Supervision
      of Factory Employees," Boston Medical and Surgical Journal,
      Vol. 176, No. 7, (February 15, 1917), pp. 239-244.

Commission on Industrial Relations, United States Senate, Final
      Report (Washington: Barnard and Miller Print, 1915), 448 pp.

Conkey, W. B., "How to Secure Employees' Loyalty," System, VIII,
      No. 1, (July, 1905), pp. 27-29.

Daugherty, Carroll R., Labor Problems in American Industry
      (Boston: Houghton, Mifflin Company, 1948), 1066 pp.

Dermody, Harold, Financial Aids to Employees (Unpublished Master's
      Thesis, Northwestern University, School of Commerce, 1940).

Douglas, Paul H., "Plant Administration of Labor," Journal of
      Political Economy, XXVII, No. 7, (July, 1919), pp. 544-
      560.

Douglas, Paul H., Real Wages in the United States, 1890-1926 (Boston: Houghton, Mifflin Company, 1930), 682 pp.

Elliott, E. Leavenworth, "Factory Lighting," American Labor Legislation Review, Vol. 1, No. 2, (June, 1911), pp. 113-116.

Feiker, F. M., "A Modern Factory Restaurant," Cassier's Magazine, XXX (June, 1906), pp. 157-160.

First National Conference on Industrial Diseases, Memorial on Occupational Diseases (A paper presented to the President of the United States on September 29, 1910).

Foote, Mark, "How the Conquerors of Business Win," System, VIII, No. 2, (August, 1905), p. 108.

Frankel, Lee K., and Fleischer, Alexander, The Human Factor in Industry (New York: The Macmillan Company, 1920), 366 pp.

Gairns, J.F., "The Promotion of Employees," Cassier's Magazine, XXXII, No. 5, (September, 1907), pp. 420-426.

Gilman, Nicholas P., A Dividend to Labor, A Study of Employers' Welfare Institutions (Boston: Houghton, Mifflin Company, 1899), 400 pp.

Gilman, Nicholas P., Profit Sharing Between Employer and Employee (Boston: Houghton, Mifflin Company, 1889), 460 pp.

Goldmark, Josephine, Fatigue and Efficiency (New York: Survey Associates, Inc., 1912), 342 pp.

Hanger, G.W.W., "Housing of the Working People in the United States," U.S. Department of Commerce and Labor, Bulletin No. 54 (Washington: Government Printing Office, September, 1904), pp. 1191-1243.

Hapgood, Herbert J., "Engaging an Employee," System, V, No. 1, (January, 1904), pp. 86-89.

Hapgood, Herbert J., "How to Secure Right Men," System, VII No. 1, (January, 1905), pp. 65-69.

Henderson, Charles R., Modern Methods of Charity (New York: The Macmillan Company, 1904), 715 pp.

Higinbotham, Harlow N., "How to Secure Employees' Loyalty," System, VIII, No. 7, (July, 1905), pp. 25-29.

Hoffman, Frederick L., "Industrial Diseases in America,"
    American Labor Legislation Review, Vol. 1, No. 1, (Jan-
    uary, 1911), pp. 35-41.

Hoffman, Frederick L., "Legal Protection from Injurious Dusts,"
    American Labor Legislation Review, Vol. 1, No. 2, (June,
    1911), pp. 110-112.

Holman, Worthington C., "A 5,000 Brain Power Organization,"
    System, VI, No. 1, (July, 1904), p. 107.

Jones, C.M., "The Employer and The Employee," System, V, No.
    5, (May, 1904), p. 349.

Jones, Edward D., The Administration of Industrial Enterprises
    (New York: Longmans Green and Company, 1920), pp. 291-
    323.

Lattimore, Alida, "Quick Lunches for Efficiency and Health," The
    Survey, XXV, (March, 1911), pp. 1012-1014.

Lippincott, Isaac, Economic Development of the United States
    (New York: D. Appleton and Company, 1921), 691 pp.

Lytle, Charles W., Wage Incentive Methods (New York: The Ronald
    Press Company, 1942), 462pp.

Morgan, Earl B., Conservation of Our Human Equipment - A Dollar
    and Cents Proposition (Paper presented before the Executive
    Committee of the National Boot and Shoe Manufacturers, Cin-
    cinnati, April 27, 1918), 8 pp.

Morrison, Samuel E., and Commager, Henry S., The Growth of the
    American Republic (New York: Oxford University Press,
    1942), 785 pp.

National Association of Employment Managers, Proceedings, First
    Annual Convention (Newark: C. Wolber Company, May, 1919),
    148 pp.

National Civic Federation, Proceedings, Conference on Welfare Work
    (New York: Andrew H. Kellogg Co., 1904), 199 pp.

National Industrial Conference Board, Employee Stock Purchase
    Plans in the United States (New York: National Industrial
    Conference Board, Inc., 1928), 245 pp.

213

Olmstead, Victor H., "The Betterment of Industrial Conditions,"
    U. S. Department of Commerce and Labor, Bulletin No. 31
    (Washington: Government Printing Office, 1900), pp. 1117-
    1156.

Parry, D. M., Disastrous Effects of a National Eight-Hour Law
    (Pamphlet, 1902).

Parkinson, Thomas I., "Problems and Progress of Workmen's
    Compensation Legislation," American Labor Legislation
    Review, Vol. 1, No. 1, (January 1911), pp. 55-71.

Peterson, Florence, Survey of Labor Economics (New York: Harper
    and Brothers, 1947), 843 pp.

Shuey, Edwin L., Factory People and Their Employers (New York:
    Lentilhon and Company, 1900), 224 pp.

Slichter, Sumner H., "Competitive Exchange as a Method of In-
    teresting Workmen in Output and Costs," American Economic
    Review, XV, No. 1, Supplement, (March, 1925), p. 94.

Slichter, Sumner H., Union Policies and Industrial Management
    (Washington: The Brookings Institution, 1941), 597 pp.

Stevens, George A., and Hatch, Leonard W., "Employers' Welfare
    Institutions," Third Annual Report of the Commissioner of
    Labor, New York State Department of Labor, (1904), pp. 225-
    329.

Stewart, Bryce M., Development of Industrial Relations in the
    United States (New York: Industrial Relations Counselors,
    Inc., 1949), 119 pp.

Thorp, Willard L., Business Annals (New York: National Bureau
    of Economic Research, Inc., 1926) 380 pp.

Tolman, William H., Industrial Betterment (New York: The Social
    Service Press, 1900), 82 pp.

Tolman, William H., Social Engineering (New York: McGraw-Hill
    Book Co., 1909), 384 pp.

United States Commissioner of Labor, "Industrial Education,"
    Twenty-fifth Annual Report (Washington: Government
    Printing Office, 1910), 822 pp.

United States Commissioner of Labor, "Trade and Technical Edu-
    cation," Seventeenth Annual Report (Washington: Govern-
    ment Printing Office, 1902), 1333 pp.

United States Commissioner of Labor, "Workmen's Insurance and
    Benefit Funds in the United States," Twenty-third Annual
    Report (Washington: Government Printing Office, 1909),
    809 pp.

United States Department of Commerce, Bureau of the Census,
    Biennial Census of Manufactures (Washington: Government
    Printing Office, 1924), 1625 pp.

United States Department of Commerce and Labor, "Cost of Living
    in the United States," Bulletin No. 93 (Washington: Govern-
    ment Printing Office, March 1911), pp. 309-570.

United States Department of Labor, Bureau of Labor Statistics,
    "Welfare Work for Employees in Industrial Establishments
    in the United States," Vol. 250 (Washington: Government
    Printing Office, February, 1919), pp. 7-139.

Wanamaker, John, "The John Wanamaker Commercial Institute,
    A Store School," The Annals, 33, No. 1, (January, 1909),
    pp. 151-154.

Wolman, Leo, The Growth of American Trade Unions, 1880-1923
    (New York: National Bureau of Economic Research, 1924),
    170 pp.

Woods, C.E., "Organizing a Factory," System, VI, No. 1, (July,
    1904), pp. 108-112.

Woytinsky, W.S. and Associates, Employment and Wages in the
    United States, The Twentieth Century Fund (Baltimore: The
    Lord Baltimore Press, 1953), 777 pp.

Wright, Chester W., Economic History of the United States (New
    York: McGraw-Hill Book Co., 1941), 1120 pp.

Zimmerman, T.J., "The System of the Armour's," System, V,
    No. 4, (April, 1904), pp. 234-247.